Exodus

INTERPRETATION
BIBLE STUDIES

Exodus

JAMES D. NEWSOME

Geneva Press
Louisville, Kentucky

Scripture quotations, unless otherwise noted, are from the New Revised Standard Version of the Bible, copyright © 1989 by the Division of Christian Education of the National Council of the Churches of Christ in the U.S.A., and are used by permission. In quotations, "Yahweh" has been substituted for "the LORD."

The photographs on pages 5, 20, 31, 37, 46, 49, 51, 74, 100, and 118 are courtesy of SuperStock, Inc. The photographs on page 15 and 61 are used by permission of Bastiaan van Elderen, The Scriptorium Center for Christian Antiquities. The photograph on page 74 is from Musée du Louvre, Paris/ET Archive, London/SuperStock. Used by permission. The photograph on page 85 is © PhotoDisc, Inc. Used by permission. The photograph on page 100 is from the Valley of the Kings, Deir el Bahri, Egypt/Donald Nuccio/SuperStock.

The illustration on page 73, by Michael Conver, is used by permission.

Book design by Drew Stevens
Cover design by Pam Poll
Cover illustration by Robert Stratton

First edition
Published by Geneva Press
Louisville, Kentucky

This book is printed on acid-free paper that meets the American National Standards Institute Z39.48 standard. ∞

PRINTED IN THE UNITED STATES OF AMERICA

98 99 00 01 02 03 04 05 06 07 — 10 9 8 7 6 5 4 3 2 1

Library of Congress Cataloging-in-Publication Data
Newsome, James D., 1931–
    Exodus / James D. Newsome. — 1st ed.
        p.   cm. — (Interpretation Bible studies)
    Includes bibliographical references.
    ISBN 0-664-50020-X (alk. paper)
    1. Bible. O.T. Exodus—Criticism, interpretation, etc.
I. Title.   II. Series.
BS1245.2.N48   1998
222′. 1207—dc21   98-38366

Contents

Series Introduction

The Bible long has been revered for its witness to God's presence and redeeming activity in the world; its message of creation and judgment, love and forgiveness, grace and hope; its memorable characters and stories; its challenges to human life; and its power to shape faith. For generations people have found in the Bible inspiration and instruction, and, for nearly as long, commentators and scholars have assisted students of the Bible. This series, Interpretation Bible Studies (IBS), continues that great heritage of scholarship with a fresh approach to biblical study.

Designed for ease and flexibility of use for either personal or group study, IBS helps readers not only to learn about the history and theology of the Bible, understand the sometimes difficult language of biblical passages, and marvel at the biblical accounts of God's activity in human life, but also to accept the challenge of the Bible's call to discipleship. IBS offers sound guidance for deepening one's knowledge of the Bible and for faithful Christian living in today's world.

IBS was developed out of three primary convictions. First, the Bible is the church's scripture and stands in a unique place of authority in Christian understanding. Second, good scholarship helps readers understand the truths of the Bible and sharpens their perception of God speaking through the Bible. Third, deep knowledge of the Bible bears fruit in one's ethical and spiritual life.

Each IBS volume has ten brief units of key passages from a book of the Bible. By moving through these units, readers capture the sweep of the whole biblical book. Each unit includes study helps, such as maps, photos, definitions of key terms, questions for reflection, and suggestions for resources for further study. In the back of each volume is a Leader's Guide that offers helpful suggestions on how to use IBS.

The Interpretation Bible Studies series grows out of the well-known Interpretation commentaries (John Knox Press), a series that helps preachers and teachers in their preparation. Although each IBS volume bears a deep kinship to its companion Interpretation commentary, IBS can stand alone. The reader need not be familiar with the Interpretation commentary to benefit from IBS. However, those who want to discover even more about the Bible will benefit by consulting Interpretation commentaries too.

Through the kind of encounter with the Bible encouraged by the Interpretation Bible Studies, the church will continue to discover God speaking afresh in the scriptures.

Introduction to Exodus

"The Easter event of the Old Testament" is a description sometimes applied to the exodus, that deliverance of the Hebrew slaves from Egyptian bondage under the leadership of Moses, the central occurrence recounted in this second book of the Bible. Easter and exodus is an apt comparison for at least these reasons: (1) By means of God's miraculous power, people are saved from an evil before which they are powerless. (2) As a result, those who have been saved enter into a new dimension of their relationship with God, a new covenant or, to be more precise, a reformulation of an existing covenant. (3) In spite of their continued sinfulness, God clings to this freshly covenanted community and they to God. (4) In their joyful acceptance of God's initiatives, the saved people assume new understandings of the trust placed in them as God's covenant people.

EXODUS שמות ואלה

1 ‏1 וְאֵ֗לֶּה שְׁמוֹת֙ בְּנֵ֣י יִשְׂרָאֵ֔ל הַבָּאִ֖ים מִצְרָ֑יְמָה אֵ֣ת יַעֲקֹ֔ב אִ֥ישׁ ס ‏2 וּבֵית֖וֹ בָּֽאוּ׃ ‏2 רְאוּבֵ֣ן שִׁמְע֔וֹן לֵוִ֖י וִיהוּדָֽה׃ ‏3 יִשָּׂשכָ֥ר זְבוּלֻ֖ן ‏4 וּבְנְיָמִֽן׃ ‏4 דָּ֥ן וְנַפְתָּלִ֖י גָּ֥ד וְאָשֵֽׁר׃ ‏5 וַיְהִ֗י כָּל־נֶ֛פֶשׁ יֹצְאֵ֥י יֶֽרֶךְ־יַעֲקֹ֖ב שִׁבְעִ֣ים נָ֑פֶשׁ וְיוֹסֵ֖ף הָיָ֥ה בְמִצְרָֽיִם׃ ‏6 וַיָּ֤מָת יוֹסֵף֙ וְכָל־אֶחָ֔יו וְכֹ֖ל הַדּ֥וֹר הַהֽוּא׃ ‏7 וּבְנֵ֣י יִשְׂרָאֵ֗ל פָּר֧וּ וַֽיִּשְׁרְצ֛וּ וַיִּרְבּ֥וּ וַיַּֽעַצְמ֖וּ בִּמְאֹ֣ד מְאֹ֑ד וַתִּמָּלֵ֥א הָאָ֖רֶץ אֹתָֽם׃ פ

"These are the names of . . ."
The beginning of the book of Exodus. From K. Elliger and W. Rudolph, eds., *Biblia Hebraica Stuttgartensia* **(Stuttgart: Deutsche Bibelgesellschaft, 1977), 86.**

Just as the New Testament is written viewing Christ's resurrection as the defining moment in God's merciful dealing with humankind (1 Cor. 15:17), the Old Testament often lifts the exodus as the measure of God's redemptive activity in Israel's life:

> Thus says the LORD,
> who makes a way in the sea,
> a path in the mighty waters,

> who brings out chariot and horse,
>   army and warrior;
> they lie down, they cannot rise,
>   they are extinguished, quenched like a wick.

(Isa. 43:16–17; compare Pss. 106:8–12; 136:10–15, and elsewhere)

In narrating this pivotal reality, the book of Exodus recounts some of the more unforgettable stories of the Old Testament: the baby Moses floating in a basket among the rushes of the Nile; God's surprising challenge to Moses from a fiery but unconsumed shrub; the safe passage of the people of Israel across the Red Sea and the immediate drowning of Pharaoh's pursuing army; God's gift of the tablets of the law; the sinful worship of a golden calf; and so on. But beyond the dramatic attraction of these engaging tales, the text weaves an account of a faithful God who engages the people at the point of their deepest need. As God delivers them, the people of Israel are pointed toward a new land, as well as a new understanding of their freedom and their responsibilities as a covenant people.

The book of Exodus is vague with respect to historical details, making precise dating of the events impossible. Nevertheless, there is little doubt that those who read this book are confronted by a genuine historical reminiscence. Like many other profound human experiences, the exodus events are too rich to be expressed in straightforward prose alone. So, in addition to narrative (chap. 14), there are also sections of poetry and song (chap. 15), codes of law (chap. 20), and formulas for worship (chaps. 25ff.). In addition, a close reading of the text indicates that more than one human hand has been at work in shaping this literature. Occasional contradictions and tensions within the text (e.g., how could only two Hebrew midwives [1:15] serve a population of more than six hundred thousand [12:37]?) permit the modern reader to see various literary origins behind the book. Yet far from detracting from the power of the book, this diversity strengthens the presentation,

---

Didn't Moses write the book of Exodus?

Perhaps Moses was the source of some of the material, but the book of Exodus as we have it today is more likely a combination of several sources. For a brief discussion of authorship and source theories, see William M. Ramsay, *The Westminster Guide to the Books of the Bible* (Louisville, Ky.: Westminster John Knox Press, 1994), 17–18; Bruce M. Metzger and Roland E. Murphy, eds., *New Oxford Annotated Bible: New Revised Standard Version* (New York: Oxford University Press, 1991), xxxv–xxxvi.

---

much as the perspectives of four different evangelists deepen our appreciation of the life, death, and resurrection of Jesus Christ.

In spite of the many-layered literary character of Exodus, the book does manifest a narrative and theological unity. The story moves forward in a clear chronological progression from the death of Joseph, through the people's encounter with God on Mount Sinai, to God's coming to dwell in the newly completed Tabernacle. As such, Exodus forms the first part of a larger chronicle (Exodus–Deuteronomy) that carries the people of God to their loss of Moses on the eve of their entry into the Land of Promise (Deuteronomy 34). Beyond that, Exodus, Leviticus, Numbers, and Deuteronomy, when prefaced by Genesis, constitute the Pentateuch, a literary formulation that appears to have been an early (c. 400 B.C.) configuration regarded as sacred scripture, with the prophetic books and the so-called Writings (Psalms, Proverbs, etc.) attaining that status somewhat later. In the Jewish tradition the first five books (Genesis–Deuteronomy) are accorded the special title Torah ("Law," "Instruction"), the most sacred and binding component of Holy Writ.

> For further readings about the book of Exodus, see Terence E. Fretheim, *Exodus,* Interpretation (Louisville, Ky.: John Knox Press, 1991); J. Gerald Janzen, *Exodus,* Westminster Bible Companion (Louisville, Ky.: Westminster John Knox Press, 1997); H. L. Ellison, *Exodus,* Daily Study Bible (Philadelphia: Westminster Press, 1982).

One way to outline the book of Exodus could be:

    1–2   Prologue; the Birth and Raising of Moses
    3–6   The Call and Commissioning of Moses
    7–11   The Plagues
  12–15   Freedom from Pharaoh
  16–18   Israel in the Sinai Desert
  19–24   The (Re)Formulation of the Covenant
  25–31   Instructions for Worship
  32–34   The People's Sinfulness and Restoration
  35–40   The Establishment of Israel's Cultic Life

Like all books of the Bible, Exodus, though fascinating from a literary and historical perspective, is primarily a statement about God and about God's saving presence in human life. Exodus is, in a word, gospel.

The gospel in Exodus contains several declarations, the most important of which may be summarized as follows: (1) The God of Israel is the Creator God who cares for the people of Israel and has chosen them as the special object of providential love. Yet even this choice of Israel is for the purpose of redeeming all creation (9:16). (2) Although the miraculous deliverance of Israel from Egyptian bondage is a new and startling initiative by God, this is the same God who has been graciously at work in the lives of Israel's ancestors. Continuity and surprise coexist in the experience of those who know God (6:2–3). (3) God's salvation of Israel is a reciprocal or covenantal relationship, one in which the people express their acceptance of God's love by certain patterns of worship and of interaction with one another (20:1–17).

Want to Know More?

About leading Bible study groups? See Roberta Hestenes, *Using the Bible in Groups* (Philadelphia: Westminster Press, 1983).

About pharaohs? See Paul J. Achtemeier, ed., *Harper's Bible Dictionary* (San Francisco: Harper & Row, 1985), 781–82.

About source theory (JEPD)? See Richard N. Soulen, *Handbook of Biblical Criticism*, 2d ed. (Atlanta: John Knox Press, 1981), 58–59, 95–97, 113–14, 134–35.

The Baby in the Basket

The story of the infant Moses set adrift on the Nile in a small papyrus boat is one of the most enduring in the Old Testament, with special appeal to children—young and old. It is a winsome narrative, of course, only because it turns out "right." The child is saved and set on his course to become God's special agent for the deliverance of Israel. Had events turned out differently, Israel's future and that of humankind would have been greatly and tragically reduced.

This brief story in 2:1–10 actually forms the climax of a chain of sinister events which begins in 1:8 with the ominous notation that "a new king arose over Egypt, who did not know Joseph." The repudiation of the one who had saved both Israel and Egypt in a previous generation (Genesis 37–50) signals a newly precarious state of affairs in the lives of Abraham's children. Pharaoh sees them as a threat to his sovereignty, and so he orders the Hebrews' enslavement under brutal and degrading conditions.

The Nile River

Pharaoh's Plot

A close reading of the text shows no record that the Hebrews had committed any seditious act or had initiated a subversive conspiracy.

Their only crime was to prosper. They prospered, and their large numbers posed a hypothetical threat in case Egypt were invaded from abroad or Pharaoh's rule were subjected to protest from within (vv. 9–10).

When Pharaoh says to his fellow Egyptians, "Let us deal shrewdly with them," we expect some clever plan for dealing with this supposed threat to the king's authority and to the peace of the kingdom. But Pharaoh's plan is anything but shrewd. Instead of weakening the Hebrews and decimating their numbers, the enslavement by Pharaoh serves only to strengthen them (v. 12). What is more, not only do the Hebrews suffer, but the character of their Egyptian masters is changed. They become fearful of their slaves (v. 12), and "ruthless" in their relations with them. (Note that the adjective is used twice, vv. 13, 14.)

This story feels authentic, not because the identity of this pharaoh is known or because these events can be pinpointed historically, but because it rings true to human nature. How many of the world's despots have drawn attention away from their own weaknesses by conjuring up some imaginary external threat to national security? The tyrant wants to generate fear and hatred toward a third party, so that perhaps his own criminality goes unnoticed.

Two Midwives

With the failure of Pharaoh's "shrewd" plan in 1:8–14, the king tries again in 1:15–22 to carry forward his scheme, this time with a more serious program of ethnic cleansing. Two midwives are brought to Pharaoh and ordered to kill all the male infants born to Hebrew women. Their names are Shiphrah and Puah (v. 15). Are these midwives Hebrews themselves? If so, Pharaoh must have been stupid to suppose that they would murder their own kind! Translators have struggled with the question as to whether the phrase in verse 15 should be "Hebrew midwives" (RSV) or "midwives to the Hebrew women" (NRSV). Either construction is a linguistic possibility. Since their names sound Hebrew, perhaps Pharaoh *is* stupid. In any event, their commission is repulsive, and the midwives refuse to execute it.

Why are there only two midwives to care for a population of Hebrew slaves "more numerous" (v. 9) than that of the Egyptians? Are these women the representatives of certain guilds of midwives? Some scholars suspect this apparent discrepancy may reveal a conflict in the traditions behind this story. Others suggest that the text reveals that Pharaoh's command was as humanly impossible for the women to carry out as it was morally impossible. Shrewd ol' Pharaoh!

The king's plan seems deficient in another respect. Why attempt a program of ethnic cleansing by killing all the *male* infants? Wouldn't the plan have a better chance to succeed by killing all the *females*? Besides, who will do Pharaoh's heavy lifting if there are no young men in the workforce?

> "The female children were considered of such little consequence as to be no threat—a striking irony, since his plan was ultimately thwarted by two Hebrew women."
> —Joyce Hollyday, *Clothed with the Sun: Biblical Women, Social Justice, and Us* (Louisville, Ky.: Westminster John Knox Press, 1994), 93.

The text bristles with irony and surprises, not the least of which is the two midwives' reason for their failure. They tell the king that Hebrew women deliver their children so quickly and effortlessly that midwifery is unneeded (v. 19). (Wouldn't *that* be nice?) It's a lie, of course, but one that appears clever enough to convince Pharaoh. The midwives' duplicity can raise a difficult question. How could God so richly bless (v. 21) those who had patently lied to the king?

Many modern readers of the book of Exodus probably conclude that a "white lie" is totally appropriate in this situation, since the lie helps thwart a terrible evil. Some refer to the midwives' lie as "creative disobedience" (Fretheim, 32).

> "Two lowly Hebrew women silence the king of Eygpt . . . with a single remark!" —Terence E. Fretheim, *Exodus*, Interpretation, 34.

Faced with a second failure, the king issues new instructions, this time to "all his people." "Every boy that is born to the Hebrews you shall throw into the Nile" (v. 22). The Nile is precisely the place where baby Moses soon finds himself (2:3), but in far different circumstances than Pharaoh intended. Another touch of irony!

The Mother of Moses

In 2:1–10 we come to the moment to which the previous verses have been leading. As often happens in the Bible, smaller units of the text are "fastened" to each other by a connecting word or phrase, in this case the references to "Nile" (1:22) and "river" (2:3, 5). But 2:1–10 is not just a continuation of the dramatic action of the preceding chapter. The narrative tightens the focus from an interest in all the Hebrew infants to one particular infant: Moses. It is as if the biblical writer(s) used the literary equivalent of a zoom lens to rivet attention to that one person whom they had in mind all along, the one by whom God will deliver the people.

The centrality of the character of Moses in the text is made evident in many ways. Of all of the persons in this brief passage, only Moses is referred to by name. We are not told the name of his parents, of his sister (although it is probably Miriam; note 15:20), or of Pharaoh's daughter. Only Moses is called by name, and his name is emphasized to show its importance (2:10—more about this below). A few chapters later, similar attention is drawn to the name of God; thus there is "much ado" about the names of the two principal persons in the book—one human, the other divine. In other words, the book of Exodus is about God and about Moses, and in their relationship lies the power to shape Israel's future. So Pharaoh is *never* named, because his power is merely illusory! And there is some justification to the fact that in the rabbinic tradition, the book of Exodus is entitled "Names," from its opening cadences: "These are the names of . . ." (1:1).

At the start, there is an announcement of Moses' priestly credentials (2:1). The reference to the Levitic descent of Moses' parents foretells Moses' future priestly functions. It is Moses the priest who will receive the tablets of the law (chap. 20:1ff.), and who will preside over the construction of the tabernacle (35:1ff.). The statement of Moses' ancestry is all too brief and fleeting, however, because of the impending danger that looms from Pharaoh's command to kill the Hebrew baby boys. When his mother can no longer conceal his existence, she prepares a "basket" for Moses to float in on the Nile.

Why put Moses in a basket in the river?

Maybe the mother of Moses was following the pharaoh's command (1:22). The Hebrew word for "basket" is possibly a loanword, from an Egyptian word that means "coffin."

Her motivation for doing this is not clear. Did she know that this spot on the river was a favorite bathing place for Pharaoh's daughter, a kindly woman who loved babies? Did she hope that any Egyptian who might discover the child would rescue him? Even though an Egyptian would face the choice between keeping him and disobeying Pharaoh, or killing him? What is clear is that she did not abandon the child. She stations his sister nearby to keep a watchful eye on the little bobbing boat.

Perhaps the early writer(s) felt that the mother's motives were irrelevant because stories of foundling children who rose to high position were common in the ancient world. A story very much like that of baby Moses in the Nile is told of the great Akkadian king Sargon (c. 2500 B.C.). As an infant, Sargon was placed in a small boat and set adrift in the Euphrates. Romulus and Remus were twin infants who were tossed into a river to drown but were nursed to health by a she-wolf and went on to establish the city of Rome.

The Hebrew word behind "basket" is used only in this story and in one other—the story of Noah, where the same Hebrew word refers to the ark (Genesis 6–8). Perhaps this choice of wording is theologically intentional, the "basket" that rescues Moses from the Nile symbolizing the great vessel that rescued Noah, his family, and the animals representing all of God's creation from the devastating flood. The original ark was the means by which humankind was saved. This present tiny "ark" will contribute to Israel's deliverance, to the benefit of all men and women everywhere!

> "Other baby boys had lost their lives in this river but Jochebed claimed it as a river of life for her son." —Joyce Hollyday, *Clothed with the Sun: Biblical Women, Social Justice, and Us* (Louisville, Ky.: Westminster John Knox Press, 1994), 117.

The Sister of Moses

The role of the sister in 2:1–10 is certainly commendable. The narrator heightens the tension in verse 4 with great skill, leaving the reader to wonder with the sister what is going to happen next. Will someone find the little ark? Will the boat drift off downstream, and into the broad sea beyond? If found, how will the finder react? The opening words of verse 5 do not allay any anxiety, just as the event as described could hardly have brought comfort to the sister: "The daughter of Pharaoh came down to bathe at the river . . ."

The sister is a brave girl. Overhearing the princess's astonished comment in recognizing a Hebrew baby, the sister approaches. (Did she suddenly pop up out of the thicket of reeds?) She wonders aloud if she can be of service in finding a wet nurse from among the Hebrew women. When given the blessing to do so, the sister goes to her own mother, whose breasts are heavy from having suckled Moses for three months, and brings her to the princess. Then the mother is given the custody of her own child and, as part of the bargain, is even paid to care for him (v. 9)!

The Daughter of Pharaoh

One suspects that the previous events are related with a wink and a nod. Unlike the portrayal of her father, the pharaoh, the portrayal of the character of the princess is more sympathetic. She is tender, intelligent, and responsive to the needs of other people. Since she was insightful enough to guess that the baby was a Hebrew, she probably would not have overlooked the fact that the girl was likely his sister, and the wet nurse, his mother. But out of compassion for the baby and his family, she pretends to be duped.

The princess loves the baby Moses and accepts him as her own. She is the one, not his birth mother, who confers on him his name. The Hebrew writers connect the name Moses to a Hebrew verb, *mashah*. *Mashah* means "to draw out" (v. 10), a precise description of the manner in which the princess saved the boy from the river. (Notice similar texts in which Moses' sons Gershom [from a word meaning "alien," Ex. 2:22] and Isaac [related to the term for "laughter," Gen. 21:1–7] are named on the basis of word plays.) However, modern scholarship now suggests that "Moses" is also an Egyptian word related to a verb meaning "to give birth to." So the princess appears to be using a rather simple device of calling the baby "Child," or "Boy."

> "If she names the child Moses because she drew him out of the water, then, whether she knows it or not, the form of the name in Hebrew, *mosheh*, identifies the child as 'the one who will draw out.' Thus, she foreshadows the child's future." —J. Gerald Janzen, *Exodus*, Westminster Bible Companion , 22.

Also of some interest is that one of ancient Egypt's most powerful rulers bore a name containing the same word-root as Moses. Thutmose III (the name means "son of Thoth," an Egyptian god) dominated the eastern Mediterranean basin barely two centuries before the appearance of the Hebrew tribes in Palestine. Very possibly the name still reverberated in Egyptian circles with overtones of power.

Several scholars have pointed to the apparent sense that the writer(s) of this story held no hostility toward the Egyptians, per se, but did feel hostile toward the despotic policies of the king and those who carried them out (note 2:11). Not only does the tenderness of the princess meet with approval, but an implied blessing is placed upon those who nurture the young Moses in Pharaoh's court (note Acts 7:22, which credits much of Moses' power to his Egyptian tutors). The openness toward persons of another culture and nationality is one of the charming aspects of the story of young Moses, and helps put into perspective the themes of liberation and civil disobedience that are prominent in the book of Exodus.

Exodus has sometimes been cited as the textbook of "liberation theology."As powerful and moving as this application can be, it is important to remember the differences between the themes of Exodus and modern liberation movements. Fretheim (18–20) calls attention to three such distinctions. (1) Although Moses once killed an Egyptian taskmaster and was confrontational in his negotiations with Pharaoh, the Israelites do not fight their way to freedom. Theirs is a deliverance won by God. (2) While there are important political and social elements in the story of the exodus, they are but part of the whole. Pharaoh is not alone as the enemy of Israel and of Israel's God—the gods of Egypt are the real forces, of whom Pharaoh is merely the human incarnation (note 12:12; 15:11; 18:11). In other words, an important cosmic dimension of the exodus must not be overlooked. And (3) the book of Exodus is not "a declaration of independence." At the Red Sea and Sinai, Israel moves from "bondage to Pharaoh to . . . bonding to Yahweh," Israel's God (Fretheim, 1).

These distinctions will return as themes throughout Exodus, but the winsome depiction of Pharaoh's daughter in 2:1–10 reminds us that the book of Exodus is not a tract of narrow political or nationalistic pamphleteering. Exodus is a statement about the redemptive power of God.

God's Presence

Among important information found in 2:1–10 (actually 1:8–2:10) is the presentation of this God who sets forth to deliver Israel. While we will encounter many facets of God's "personality" throughout Exodus, here the subtlety with which God goes about God's business is impressive. There are no dramatic encounters in this passage, no sudden interventions by God upon the human scene. In fact, an idle reading of the text might lead one to conclude that God is not present at all.

But that would be a misreading. The God who is present in the opening narratives of Exodus is a God who influences events indirectly. The infant Hebrew males are saved not because God held back the murderous hands of the midwives, as God would later roll back the Red Sea. They were saved because the midwives "feared" the God who valued the babies' lives (note that the statement is made twice, 1:17, 21). The nearest God comes to direct intervention is to deal "well" with the midwives (1:20), and reward them with large families (1:21).

Yet subtle evidence is there for those who know the larger story. When Pharaoh's daughter lifts Moses out of the reeds of the Nile marsh and when she later provides him with the security of the royal court, God's will has been done. The God of Exodus is a God who can whisper, as well as shout.

> ### Is God absent?
>
> God speaks or is mentioned in every chapter of Exodus except 37–39. For such a prominent character in the book of Exodus, God has a surprisingly low profile in this passage. For a thorough discussion on this topic, see Donald E. Gowan, *Theology in Exodus: Biblical Theology in the Form of a Commentary* (Louisville, Ky.: Westminster John Knox Press, 1994), 1–24.

The Purpose of the Story

The themes of creation and promise, prominent in Genesis, continue here. As noted above, the Hebrew term used for the papyrus basket in which Moses floats in the river has theological significance. So we may presume that both the creation poem in Genesis 1:1–2:4 and God's statement to Noah in Genesis 9:11 ("Never again shall there be a flood to destroy the earth") stand as a backdrop to the present text.

The theme of God's promise in creation stands in tension with another theme in Genesis, that of the persistent threat to God's redemptive purpose imposed by human sinfulness and evil. For example, hardly has God called Abraham and promised to bless all humankind through his family (Gen. 12:1–3) than Abraham willingly endangers the safety of his wife Sarah in order to save his own skin (12:10–16). Later, the promise is endangered again when Isaac's sons quarrel because Jacob has stolen the blessing that belonged to his brother, Esau (Genesis 27). The promise is imperiled again and again.

In Exodus 2:1–10, the sinful threat comes not from within but from without, in the form of Pharaoh's malevolent designs. Just as God saved the divine promise to Israel and to humankind in the days of Israel's earliest ancestors, so God does again. When the princess deals kindly with the baby in the river, Pharaoh's evil is thwarted. God's creative and redemptive purposes move forward again. Though the creative energies of God and the sinful will of humans continue to clash, God's compassionate governance of the world is not defeated.

An Anticipation of Jesus

Another feature of theological importance is the connection between the infancy of Moses and that of Jesus. Clearly, the story of the birth of Jesus in Matthew's Gospel was written with Exodus 2:1–10—and indeed the larger exodus experience—in mind. The figure of Pharaoh and that of Herod are strikingly similar: both are autocrats; both threaten the life not only of a single infant but of an entire generation; and both have their evil intents overturned by God. Matthew even borrows a prophetic text from the Old Testament which celebrates the exodus event (Hos. 11:1), and applies it to the young Jesus' return from Egypt (Matt. 2:15).

Like Moses, Jesus is the one on whom all God's plans for human deliverance are pinned. As noted above, the narratives in 1:8–14 and 1:15–22 move from considering all of imperiled Israel to "zero in" (2:1–10) on the sole figure of Moses as the one who will be God's instrument of deliverance. In a similar way, the New Testament focuses on Jesus as God's redeemer of humankind, the lone (and sometimes lonely) agent of God's salvation.

The story of Moses anticipates that of Jesus in many ways. Both men are born in the midst of a people who are suffering under the tyranny of an evil ruler. Both escape death that is intended for their whole infant generation. Both end up fulfilling God's will for their lives only after much suffering. (The nature of Moses' suffering differs from that of Jesus, as Moses' death is not in and of itself considered redemptive.) Both experience a period of exile in the wilderness. Both endure misunderstanding and repudiation by those who are closest to them.

 Want to Know More?

About irony? See George Arthur Buttrick, ed., *The Interpreter's Dictionary of the Bible*, vol. 2 (Nashville: Abingdon Press, 1962), 726–28.

About midwives? See Buttrick, ed., *The Interpreter's Dictionary of the Bible*, vol. 3, 377.

About papyrus? See Paul J. Achtemeier, ed., *Harper's Bible Dictionary* (San Francisco: Harper & Row, 1985), 746–47.

About the role of women in Old Testament times? See Carol A. Newsom and Sharon H. Ringe, editors, *Women's Bible Commentary*, Expanded Edition (Louisville, Ky.: Westminster John Knox Press, 1998), 251–59; for an excellent, very readable treatment, see Evelyn and Frank Stagg, *Woman in the World of Jesus* (Philadelphia: Westminster Press, 1978).

Like Jesus, Moses is in conflict with the authorities at birth, and the conflict is renewed in his adulthood. The conflict, though, isn't a mere mismating of personalities. Rather, the conflict is part of a cosmic struggle to redeem the children of Israel. From an inauspicious beginning in a small ark, the story turns out more "right" than could ever be imagined. Through Moses, the people of Israel gain freedom, a renewed covenant with God, and a new home in a promised land.

? Questions for Reflection

1. This story is not just about Moses but also about several women. Who are the women of this story? Why are these women mentioned? What is their relationship to Moses? What risks do they take? What risks can people today take on account of the faith?
2. The theme of God's promise is highlighted in this story. What are some of the ways God's promise is seen in this story? How are they similar to and different from those seen in other places in the Bible? What promises of God carry over into today?
3. The presence of God is very much "behind the scenes" in this passage. What does this passage offer to your understanding of God's providence for the world? What are ways God's presence can be clearly seen? How is God's presence invisible?
4. The narratives of Exodus were probably transmitted orally before anything was written down. When the women get the best of Pharaoh in this passage, one can almost hear the chuckles, or sense the elbows in the ribs of the hearers of this story. What are some of the ironies of this passage? How does noting these ironies shape your understanding of this passage?

2

The Call of Moses

What happens to Moses from the time he is taken into Pharaoh's court as a small child until he reemerges as the champion of the Hebrew's cause? The book of Exodus is largely silent on this question. In the New Testament, this same pattern of silence is observed by the four evangelists in the story of Jesus. There, too, almost no information is given about Jesus' experiences between infancy and adulthood. (The major exception is Luke 2:40–52.)

However, a little information about Moses' life in this period can be gleaned from suggestions and hints here and there in the text. Moses apparently is deeply "Egyptianized," at least in terms of externals (clothing, speech, or manner). After Moses' first meeting with the daughters of the Midianite priest Jethro, the women report to their father that "an Egyptian helped us" (2:19). So Moses must have looked or acted Egyptian. Yet, whatever elements of Egyptian culture he may have absorbed, Moses is at heart a Hebrew,

Jebel Katarin, one of the sites traditionally associated with Mount Sinai

and he will not forget his Hebrew heritage. His blood boils when he sees one of the Egyptian overseers of the labor gangs beating a Hebrew worker, "one of his kinsfolk" (2:11). Chapter 3 begins with

Moses having murdered the Egyptian and fled into the desert of Midian.

During Moses' time in the desert of Midian (possibly a parallel is Jesus' time in the wilderness [compare Mark 1:12–13, Matt. 4:1–11, Luke 4:1–13], but with significant differences) several important events occur. First, Moses marries Jethro's daughter Zipporah, and they have a son (2:21–22). Also, the pharaoh, Moses' adoptive grandfather, dies back in Egypt. Instead of bringing relief to the enslaved Hebrews, Pharaoh's death appears to deepen their misery all the more (2:23). The one positive consequence of Pharaoh's death is a renewed undertaking by God to deliver the suffering people (2:24). What God is about to do now in Israel's life is linked to what God had done before. "God remembered his covenant with Abraham, Isaac, and Jacob," and this reality underscores the continuity between this new act of deliverance and God's providential care of the ancestors of the Hebrews. This is no new god whom Moses is about to meet, but the very same God who has guided the Hebrews in earlier generations. The covenant at Sinai is not a new covenant, but a renewal of the covenant with Abraham and Sarah (Gen. 15:1–20, 17:1–22).

The Burning Bush

The encounter between God and Moses at the burning bush (3:1ff.), like the story of the baby in the basket, is another narrative from Exodus that has fascinated readers over the centuries with its dramatic intensity. The site is Mount Horeb, probably the same spot referred to elsewhere in the text as Mount Sinai (the word "Horeb" is related to a Hebrew term meaning "waste" or "desert").

> The Hebrew term here for bush, *seneh* [3:2] sounds very much like "Sinai," which is possibly one factor in the Horeb-Sinai identification. The precise location of this mountain is unknown. One of the possible sites is Jebel Musa, "Mountain of Moses," where modern tours are conducted.

Even before the time of Moses, Horeb might have been a sacred spot, or a place of worship of local deities and jinns (powerful spirits) of the desert. Perhaps Horeb was a shrine presided over by Jethro in his role as Midianite priest, which could account for Moses' presence there in his capacity as Jethro's shepherd. The text is silent on these details other than to call Horeb "the mountain of God" (v. 1). The "layering" of holy places, establishing a new place of worship on the site of an older one, is a common feature of many human cultures, so Moses' experience here may be part of a long tradition of worship carried out on the site. (Notice the large number of Christian churches in Europe built on previously "pagan" sites, or the location of the cathedral in Mexico City on the site of a prominent Aztec sanctuary.)

If Horeb was not a sacred spot already, then this event is even more unexpected. To be sure, Moses acts initially as if an encounter with God is the last thing on his mind. At first, the sight of the bush being burned, but not consumed, is just a visual curiosity for Moses. Only when he hears God's voice does he understand this curiosity to be an appearance of God, a theophany. (The statement in verse 2, "There the angel of the LORD appeared to him in a flame," probably means that the fire was the result of angelic activity, not that Moses actually saw an angel. If he had seen an angel, he probably would have reacted to the fire with more awe and less curiosity.)

In addressing Moses, God makes two declarations. First, this site is a holy one, and Moses must acknowledge the presence of the numinous and supernatural by removing his shoes (compare Joshua 5:15, and note the similarity to the Muslim requirement that shoes must be removed before entering a mosque). Second, the divine presence in the burning-but-unconsumed bush is no desert jinn, but the ancestral God of the Hebrews, "the God of Abraham, the God of Isaac, and the God of Jacob" (v. 6, compare 2:24). As in other places in the Bible, the book of Exodus emphasizes both continuity and newness in the events taking place in the life of Moses and of Israel. As he encountered this awesome presence, Moses hid his face because he believed that no one could look God in the face and live. (Compare 33:20. Notice also that in Isa. 6:2 even the seraphim shield their faces from holy God.)

> "Where and why do we wear shoes? . . . Footwear protects us from the ground, and it renders us insensitive to what our soles (and our souls!) might feel there." —J. Gerald Janzen, *Exodus*, Westminster Bible Companion, 28.

Moses' Protests

God's appearance in the burning bush is not an end in itself; it is only the initial step in God's call to Moses. Moses is to be the divine agent in setting the Hebrew slaves free. God, who is suffering over the plight of the captives, pours out concern in a declaration

(3:7–10), and this divine compassion comes to a climax in the summons to Moses: "So come, I will send you to Pharaoh to bring my people, the Israelites, out of Egypt" (v. 10).

The First Protest

God is persistent, for this is the first of several refusals by Moses. In this instance, Moses protests that he is not sufficiently important or worthy to carry out such an enormous commission: "Who am I that I should go to Pharaoh, and bring the Israelites out of Egypt?" (3:11).

God answers Moses' objection in words that have caused readers over the centuries to scratch their heads in puzzlement. When God responds that "this shall be the sign for you that it is I who sent you" (v. 12), one is left wondering what is meant by "this." In other words, *what* sign? Perhaps "this" refers back to the burning bush, or ahead to the future when Moses will lead the people out of Egypt. Yet in spite of this uncertainty, one element in God's statement is quite clear: "I will be with you." God promises to be present with Moses, and when all is said and done, Moses will need God's presence for the fulfillment of his commission.

The Second Protest

Moses still is not convinced. He objects a second time. His remarks are something like: "When I tell my fellow Israelites that a God has sent me (Egypt, after all, is a land of many gods), they will want to know your name. What shall I tell them?" (v. 13, paraphrased).

Earlier in Exodus, the significance of the name "Moses" was mentioned (2:10), and here the biblical text addresses the question of the name of the other principal character of the book of Exodus. Why does Moses raise the question of God's name? Does Moses himself want to know? Or does he genuinely wish to be able to answer the question of the people? Or is he simply stalling before taking on a terrible responsibility? The answer is not clear, but in any event, in the ancient world, to know someone's name was to know something of the essence of that person. Thus, to know the name of God is to know something deep about the nature of God. Regardless of Moses' motivation, then, to ask for God's name is a momentous question.

God replies in words that are as baffling as they are reassuring: "I AM WHO I AM . . . Thus you shall say to the Israelites, 'I AM has sent me'" (3:14). God's self-disclosure of the divine name entails enormous consequences. For God to reveal something of the divine nature makes God vulnerable to both Moses and the Israelites. A

person who reveals intimate personal knowledge to another yields power to that other person. Just so, when God yields the divine name, God surrenders some power. Without some degree of surrendered intimacy, though, trusting relationships are not possible. When God complies with Moses' request for a name, God establishes a relationship of trust with Moses, a bond that proves indispensable in the tasks that lie ahead and forms the basis for the covenant to be renewed.

> The NRSV translates the Hebrew text of the divine name, Yahweh, with "LORD"—four capital letters. This understanding of the translation helps reveal the word play in verse 15. Another Hebrew term that means something like "master" or "sovereign" also occurs with reference to God. In these instances, the NRSV uses "Lord." (Note the use of both "LORD" and "Lord" in Ex. 4:10.) The translation "Jehovah" arose during the Middle Ages through a misunderstanding of the pronunciation of Yahweh, and is not a true linguistic form.

What does God's reply mean? What sort of name is "I AM WHO I AM?" Scholars have debated this question for generations, but there is no easy answer. Many agree that a connection exists between the phrase "I am" and the personal name of the God of Israel, Yahweh. In the first place, the term Yahweh sounds very much like the basic form of the Hebrew verb "to be," *hayah*. Perhaps the reply means that the God of Israel is associated with the idea of "being" or "is-ness." Another possible meaning is an affirmation that the God of Israel is Creator—the God who brings all things into being. Or perhaps the intention is that this God is the one who alone truly exists, who alone truly "is," and upon whose existence all other persons and things depend for their own existence. Maybe "I AM WHO I AM" simply means "I am beyond description." "I am who I am, and beyond that nothing more may be said."

The text also links "I am" with the name of God, Yahweh. No sooner has the divine name been revealed as "I am" than God continues, "Say to the Israelites, 'Yahweh, the God of your ancestors . . . has sent me to you'" (v. 15). "I am" and "Yahweh" are one and the same, the God of Abraham, Isaac, and Jacob. Again, newness and continuity go hand in hand.

The Third Protest

Moses raises a third objection, and this time the issue is trust. Perhaps Moses is convinced that *he* can trust this God who appeared so dramatically in the flaming bush, but the people might not. Will telling them that Moses knows God's name mute any suspicions they may have? Even if he tells them exactly what God has said to him? So Moses projects a hypothetical scenario that would haunt anyone in his position. "But suppose," he challenges God, "they [the people] do not believe me or listen to me, but say 'Yahweh did not appear to you'"(4:1). Implied is the question, What do I do then?

Perhaps the question posed by one of the two Hebrews whose earlier quarrel Moses had attempted to mediate now rings in the inner recess of his mind: "Who made you a ruler and judge over us?" (2:14). Moses was never elected by a tribal council of the Hebrews to be their leader. In many ways he was an outsider. Most of his life was spent in Pharaoh's court and in the family of the Midianite priest Jethro. Except for brief periods, he had never lived among the people he is being sent back to lead. Even though *he* trusts Yahweh, why should the people trust him or a God he claims to represent?

Yahweh responds to this third objection with understanding and compassion for Moses' situation. God does not reproach Moses or show any sign of impatience, although that will come later (Num. 20:10–13). Instead Yahweh arms Moses with three miraculous weapons or signs, three "magic tricks" that will dazzle the Hebrews so they can harbor no doubts that Moses is who he claims to be: the servant of the God of Israel. Moses' staff is turned into a snake and back into a staff (4:2–4). Moses' hand is made leprous, then healthy again (4:6–8). And Moses is promised the power to turn water from the Nile into blood, although this latter feat is not performed at the moment—presumably because Moses is still out in the desert of Midian (4:9).

Yahweh's reaction is an appropriate response to the context of Moses and the Hebrews in Egypt. The ancient Egyptians put great faith in works of magic. Many a magical charm could be spoken to guard against harmful threats. One magical incantation from ancient Egypt is interesting for both the preoccupation with a malevolent snake and the power of a name:

> Words to be spoken: "Back with thee, hidden snake. Hide thyself! Thou shalt not make King Unis see thee. Back with thee, hidden snake! Hide thyself! Thou shalt not come to the place where King Unis is lest he tell that name of thine against thee. . . . Turn about, turn about! O monster, lie down!" (Pritchard, 326)

Notice the threefold imperative directed against the snake. The idea of three carried magical implications in the ancient world. For example, Moses is given three signs. Exodus refers several times to Pharaoh's magicians and their skills in the arts of conjuring (7:22 and elsewhere). Surely the Hebrews were influenced by the confidence of their Egyptian captors in magic.

Moses' magic tricks seem to serve several purposes. The signs not only affirm the supremacy of the God of Israel over the gods of Egypt, but also confirm for the Hebrews that it is their God who has spoken to Moses. Yahweh states the purpose of the powers at Moses' disposal: ". . . so that they [the Hebrews] may believe that Yahweh, the God of their ancestors, the God of Abraham, the God of Isaac, the God of Jacob, has appeared to you" (4:5). (Once again the familiar formula is presented, connecting these new experiences to Israel's encounters with God in the past.) The signs also anticipate the plagues that later Yahweh will impose on the Egyptians (the first plague, water turned to blood; the second, frogs; the sixth, boils).

The Fourth Protest

Still Moses resists and now raises a fourth objection. "I'm not very good on my feet, Lord," is one paraphrase of 4:10. "I never have been a good public speaker, and not even your meeting me in this strange fashion out here in the desert has changed that fact. I am still 'slow of speech and slow of tongue.'" Anyone who has found terror in standing before a group and making a speech can identify with Moses. Unfortunately, God is not calling Moses to address the local Kiwanis Club or the town council, but Pharaoh—the most powerful man on earth! No wonder he feels inadequate. Who wouldn't?

More may be involved here than a simple case of bad stage fright. Some scholars suggest that Moses has a speech defect. If that is the case, it would only heighten Moses' fear. The weakness of Moses both underscores and previews Paul's words about Christ—that God chose to work not through the powerful of the world but through the weak and lowly (1 Cor. 1:26–27).

God replies again patiently, but forcefully, as a teacher might speak to a student. When all is said and done, isn't this God the same Creator God (one of the possible meanings of the name Yahweh)? Didn't God provide humans with the power of their senses, including human speech? "Is it not I, Yahweh?" (4:11). The God who calls Moses is the God who promises to be Moses' lips and tongue.

> **Did Moses stammer?**
>
> Moses' description of himself is unclear. Is he being humble? (see Num. 12:3). Or is there a physical problem? No other indication is given in scripture. An irony of the story is that if he did stammer, he was nonetheless able to engage God in a long discussion and communicate quite well.

Now all of Moses' defenses have been stripped away. He is out of excuses. Still he is terrified, and who wouldn't be? Instead of objecting to God a fifth time, Moses tries entreaty. "O my Lord, please send someone else" (4:13), which could mean either "please send someone instead of me" or "please send someone along with me."

For the first time Yahweh gets angry (4:14). What else could God say or do to convince Moses that he is God's chosen? But even in anger, God is sympathetic to Moses' state of mind. Yahweh promises Moses that his brother Aaron will be at his side. Aaron will help because he "can speak fluently." Only now does Moses agree to God's call and accept the staff with which the "signs" are to be accomplished (4:17). Only now does he ask Jethro's permission to return to Egypt (4:18).

> "Both God and Moses recognize that God is not demystified through further understanding. In fact, the more one understands God, the more mysterious God becomes. God is the supreme examplification of the old adage: The more you know, the more you know you don't know." —Terence E. Fretheim, *Exodus*, Interpretation, 62–63.

The Nature of God

An interesting feature of this passage is God's patient persistence. The burning bush and the magical staff are impressive, to be sure, but neither reveals the nature of God as dramatically as the manner in which God responds to Moses' protests. In each case, God takes what Moses has to say with utmost seriousness. Does Moses feel himself unworthy? God promises to accompany him. Does Moses need to know the name of God? Here it is: "I am." Does Moses fear that the people will not have confidence in him? God arms him with certain powers of magic. Does Moses stammer? God will be his mouth. Is Moses still afraid to face Pharaoh alone? God will send Aaron along to accompany him.

This seems to say very strongly that God may call women and men to undertake tasks that seem much too large to accomplish. But just as God promises to work with the person in the accomplishment of those tasks, God also understands the fear and self-doubt that remain in the heart of even the most committed person.

Many scholars note that Moses' resistance to God's call and God's response to his resistance are similar to the experiences of important prophetic figures of a later time. Isaiah is an example. That prophet's encounter with God (Isa. 6:1–13) must have been even more terrifying than Moses' encounter at the burning bush. In Isaiah's case, a group of otherworldly six-winged creatures called seraphs (angels?) are in attendance. There is an actual vision of God, or at least of the hem of royal garments—a God who is "high and lofty." There is the chant of the seraphs: "Holy, holy, holy is Yahweh of hosts; the whole earth is full of his glory."

Frightened? Of course he was. And he was overwhelmed by a sense of his own mortality and sinfulness. So Isaiah cries, "Woe is me. I am lost. I am a man of unclean lips." For how could a man whose lips are sinful speak the words of a holy God?

God responds by having one of the flying creatures take a hot coal from the Temple altar and place it against Isaiah's mouth. "Now that this has touched your lips," Yahweh declares, ". . . your sin is blotted out." With this, Isaiah answers God's call to the prophetic office. If this newly ordained prophet were still conscious of trembling knees, who could blame him?

Jeremiah is another example. The account of Jeremiah's initial encounter with God (Jer. 1:4–10) is not as rich

 Want to Know More?

About covenant? See Donald K. McKim, *Westminster Dictionary of Theological Terms* (Louisville, Ky.: Westminster John Knox Press, 1996), 64; Gordon S. Wakefield, *The Westminster Dictionary of Christian Spirituality* (Philadelphia: Westminster Press, 1983), 98–99; Werner H. Schmidt, *Faith of the Old Testament: A History* (Philadelphia: Westminster Press, 1983), 106–9.

About magic? See McKim, *Westminster Dictionary of Theological Terms*, 166; Paul J. Achtemeier, ed., *Harper's Bible Dictionary* (San Francisco: Harper & Row, 1985), 594–96.

About other references to "I am"? Jesus borrows the phrase repeatedly in John 6:35; 8:12; 10:7, 11; 11:25; 14:6; 15:1. See the discussion in Ben Witherington, III, *John's Wisdom: A Commentary on the Fourth Gospel* (Louisville, Ky.: Westminster John Knox Press, 1995), 156–58.

with detail as that of Isaiah, but the similarities are striking. Yahweh tells Jeremiah that he was ordained to be a prophet even before he was conceived in the womb (1:5)—a sobering thought that leaves Jeremiah little room to negotiate with God. But like Moses and Isaiah, Jeremiah does not assume the prophetic office willingly. "Ah, Lord GOD! Truly I do not know how to speak, for I am only a boy" (Jer. 1:6). God brushes aside Jeremiah's concern using words similar to those directed to Moses in Exodus 4:12. Yahweh says in effect, "I will tell you what you are to say."

Then Jeremiah reports an action that parallels the seraph's deployment of a hot coal in Isaiah 6:

> Then Yahweh put out his hand and touched my mouth; and Yahweh said to me,
>
> > Now I have put my words in your mouth.
> > See, today I appoint you over nations and over kingdoms,
> > to pluck up and to pull down,
> > to destroy and to overthrow,
> > to build and to plant. (Jer. 1:9–10)

(Compare Ezek. 3:1–3, where that prophet is offered a scroll to eat, a document that represents the word of God. The association of the word of God with the mouth of the prophet is an enduring one in the Old Testament.)

God's command that Moses should return to Pharaoh to demand freedom for the Hebrew slaves would terrify even the most stouthearted. Moses' attempt to erect roadblocks in the path is not surprising. What is wonderfully astonishing is that God deals both mercifully and powerfully with this unwilling servant. God overcomes the objections of Moses and invests him with strength for performing the awesome tasks that lie ahead.

? Questions for Reflection

1. This story emphasizes both newness and continuity. God is about to do something dramatically new to redeem the Hebrew slaves, but this new thing has common features with the way God has acted in the past to protect "Abraham, Isaac, and Jacob," and the other ancestors of the Hebrews. How do you see this same dynamic of newness and continuity in other events in the Bible—the resurrection of Jesus, for example? How can this be seen in the way God acts in life today?

2. Moses raised four protests, or objections, to God's call. In what ways are the objections of contemporary people to God's call similar to Moses' protests? In what ways are they different?

3. Dramatic changes happen in the life of Moses in this story. What would you do if such changes happened to you?

4. There is a sense of wonder and unexpectedness in this passage. Moses was out, keeping his flock, when unexpectedly, the angel of the Lord appeared to him. Two questions: What are some of the wonders and unexpected aspects about this passage? What are some of the parallels that you see between the life of Moses and that of Jesus?

3 Exodus 7:1–24

The First Plague

Chapter 7 of Exodus divides logically into three sections: renewal of the commission (vv. 1–7), prelude to the plagues (vv. 8–13), and water turned to blood (vv. 14–24). In the same way that the first two sections set the stage for the third, all of chapter 7 introduces chapters 7–12, the story of the ten plagues and the first Passover. So each section is a story, but also a part of a larger story, which, in turn, is part of an even larger story.

A Renewal of Moses' Commission from God

Verses 1–7 repeat what God said earlier to Moses, both by way of commission and of promise. Beginning at 3:10, God had repeated that Moses was to be God's agent to free the Israelites. Even though this commission was softened when God allowed Moses' brother Aaron to be at his side as spokesman, the commission to Moses continued.

Exodus 7:1–7 does not simply re-state previous material; the language used here is considerably bolder. Moses is now described, in the NRSV translation, as "like God to Pharaoh" (7:1), or, as the Jerusalem Bible reads: "I have made you as a god for Pharaoh." And Aaron is "your *navi*," a Hebrew term by which the Old Testament usually refers to the great "classical" prophets like Amos, Hosea, Isaiah, or Jeremiah. Moses is portrayed not just as God's agent but as

> "Getting Pharaoh's attention is not his task; he is ordered rather to speak what Yahweh speaks. Yahweh has plans of his own for getting and holding Pharaoh's attention."
> —John I. Durham, *Exodus*, Word Biblical Commentary, 86.

26

the actual embodiment of the divine presence. The relationship between Moses and Aaron is portrayed as being like the relationship
between God and the great prophets to come—the ones who declare
the divine will. Since Moses was already afraid (note 6:30), this language must have increased his terror.

The text has finished speaking of Moses' fear, however. From now
on, Moses is portrayed as resolute and firm. He is now a person who,
once his reservations have been put aside, stands faithful to respond
to whatever God has called him to do. Not till later, when he is faced
with criticism from his own people, will Moses waver again (Ex.
17:1–7).

Hardening the Pharaoh's Heart

Verses 1–7 contain one of the most troubling statements in all the
book of Exodus. Moses and Aaron will indeed confront Pharaoh
with the demand that the Israelites be released from their bondage
(7:2). In time, the captives will find
their freedom, as a result of God's intervention in their lives (7:4–5). But
between those two events lies a series
of struggles and bitter disappoint-
ments for the Israelites, and widespread ruin and death for the
Egyptians. The reason is that "I
(Yahweh) will harden Pharaoh's
heart" (v. 3).

This verse presents a major theological question: Why would God
motivate someone to sin, then turn
around and punish that person for
committing the sin? At best, God's
behavior seems illogical. At worst,
such behavior appears sadistic. On a
more practical level, assuming that
God wants the Israelites to be free,
why would God cause Pharaoh to be an obstruction?

> **The condition of Pharaoh's heart?**
>
> Throughout the book of Exodus, the hard-
> ening of Pharaoh's heart is mentioned. In
> places, as here in 7:3, God hardens
> Pharaoh's heart (see also 9:12; 10:1;
> 14:8). In others, Pharaoh hardens his own
> heart (8:15, 32; 9:34). In still others,
> Pharaoh's heart is hardened, but the
> phrase is stated passively without naming
> an active agent (7:22; 8:19; 9:7). Three
> distinct Hebrew words are used among the
> eighteen references, but all are translated
> identically in English as "hardened." One
> word describes something hard as rock (as
> in 9:12), another describes something dif-
> ficult or severe (as in 7:3), and the third de-
> scribes something burdensome or heavy
> (as in 8:15).

The Old Testament faces a similar question elsewhere. In 2
Samuel 24, an angry Yahweh orders King David to take a census of

the people. Then David gets punished, presumably because the census led to the authoritarian policies of his son Solomon. When this same story is retold in 1 Chronicles 21, the role of "Yahweh" (2 Sam. 24:1) is replaced with "Satan" (1 Chron. 21:1). The question of why God would punish someone for doing something commanded by God is removed by a stroke of the pen. Instead, Satan becomes the culprit. But the plague stories are not retold later in the Bible. As the text stands, God seems to punish Pharaoh and the Egyptians for something for which God is ultimately responsible.

From earliest times commentators and interpreters of the text have wrestled with this issue without clear success. (1) Some have explained 7:3 in psychological terms—perhaps Pharaoh proved himself obstinate in the face of Moses' demands because of his own emotions and twisted logic. Some texts within the cycle of plague stories suggest this possibility, but verses like 7:3 seem to say something else entirely. (2) Others read the text theologically, and see a statement regarding divine predestination or God's foreknowledge. In this understanding, Pharaoh seems to be a puppet. (3) Still others suggest that 7:3 reflects the historical development of the text. A later writer is explaining an earlier tradition that told of a series of supernatural signs, which failed to achieve their purpose (Childs, 174). But this literary-historical view—while perhaps true—does not resolve the difficulty presented to readers by the text as presently composed. (4) Others attempt to blend elements of the above explanations, so as to maximize their strengths and minimize their weaknesses (see Fretheim, 96ff.).

All of these approaches to 7:3 should be taken seriously, but even with their help, the problematic nature of the verse remains—one of many "sticky" texts in the Old Testament. (Exodus poses other "sticky" texts. Consider Ex. 4:24–26. Why would Yahweh want to kill Moses? And, if Yahweh wanted to kill Moses, why be deterred by Zipporah's magic in 4:25?)

> "The truth lies not so much in the signs themselves as in what the signs point to: 'You shall know that I am the Lord your God' (6:7). . . . All is told in order that we, like pharaoh, will learn [this]." —William M. Ramsay, *The Westminster Guide to the Books of the Bible* (Louisville, Ky.: Westminster John Knox Press, 1994), 44.

One thing should be noted, however, which may help put the matter in perspective. The various texts that speak of Pharaoh's hardening of heart are closely associated with the "signs." Yahweh provides the signs for Pharaoh's eyes so that the king will take Moses' demands seriously (note that association in 7:3). The whole encounter between Moses and

Pharaoh is *really* a contest between Yahweh and Pharaoh. Or more precisely, the contest is between Yahweh and the gods of Egypt—a power struggle to determine who is in control of human affairs. Of course, Yahweh will ultimately prevail, and perhaps 7:3—regardless of the problematic nature—is an important means by which the text declares Yahweh's ultimate sovereignty over all life. Exodus 7:5 affirms this perspective. When the matter is finally settled, "the Egyptians shall know that I am Yahweh." Pharaoh's struggle is with the sovereign Lord of all creation. (Paul's comment on the matter in Romans 9:17–18 is of considerable interest, as noted below under "The Water Turned to Blood.")

A Prelude to the Plagues

Verses 8–13 begin the narrative cycle of the ten plagues. Though there is no plague involved in these verses, the "action" described may be characterized as a kind of dress rehearsal for what lies ahead.

Yahweh anticipated that Pharaoh would demand credentials at the appearance by Moses and Aaron before him. Like any Egyptian who comes before Pharaoh, Moses and Aaron will be asked to produce a "wonder." They will need magical proof that they are who they claim to be, representatives of God.

> "Yahweh is concerned to bring the Pharaoh to an experiential knowledge of *his* powerful Presence, not of Moses' truthfulness or Aaron's eloquence." —John I. Durham, *Exodus*, Word Biblical Commentary, 86–87.

The transformation of the staff into a snake has been anticipated in Exodus 4:1–5, but an awesome new element is now introduced. In 4:3, the Hebrew term translated "snake" is one of several Hebrew words that refer to the suborder of the reptile class called Serpentes, or "ordinary" snakes. But here in chapter 7 (vv. 9, 10, 12) the term *tannin* is used, which is sometimes translated "dragon" or "monster" (note Jer. 51:34). Without a doubt, *tannin* is a reference to the same mythological creature that appears in the creation stories of many of ancient Israel's neighbors. The Egyptian sorcerers also create dragons out of their staffs. This clash is not merely one of political wills, but a battle of cosmological import. It is Yahweh versus the gods of Egypt. As a foreshadowing of who will win this cosmic battle, Aaron's staff swallows the staffs of Pharaoh's magicians.

In Exodus 15:12, the waters of the Red Sea swallow Pharaoh's armies. That a common Hebrew term translated "swallow" in 7:12

is used only here and in 15:12 in all of Exodus indicates that the writers see this incident as anticipating God's dramatic victory at the Red Sea. What irony—Pharaoh asks for a wonder and receives not only the sign of the staff-become-a-dragon but also a subtle indication of the ultimate demise of his army. Of course, he is blind to both.

> "When 'everybody' throws down his staff and Pharaoh's palace is about to be overrun with monstrous snakes, Aaron's staff 'gobbled up' or 'gulped down' everybody else's staff." —John I. Durham, *Exodus*, Word Biblical Commentary, 92.

The Water Turned to Blood

Verses 14–24 reveal what will become a succession of ten plagues sent by God to convince Pharaoh to let Israel go. Unlike the passover or the miraculous crossing of the Red Sea, which are recalled frequently elsewhere (compare Ps.136:10–15), the imagery of the ten plagues is almost never referred to elsewhere in the Bible. Childs (162–64), for example, points to only two places in the New Testament where there is a reference to the narrative cycle of the plagues: Romans 9:17, where Paul makes reference to the hardening of Pharaoh's heart, and Revelation 8 and 16, where plagues are described as marking the end time. No clear reason exists for this lack of interest elsewhere in the Bible concerning the plague stories.

The first plague was foreshadowed in 4:9. As noted previously, this is the third of three signs (4:1–9) whose intent was to persuade Moses that God had empowered him to convince the Israelites to follow Moses' leadership. Unlike the first two signs, the staff-become-a-snake and Moses' hand turned leprous, this sign is not previewed in Exodus 4 but is a promise that God's power through Moses can turn the waters of the Nile into blood.

The account of the first plague is in a narrated form that continues in the other plague stories. There is an initial statement about the hardening of Pharaoh's heart (7:14), followed by Moses' declaration that Pharaoh must let the Israelites go (7:16). Then the plague occurs (7:19–21) as a miraculous event ordered by God and performed by Moses and Aaron. In many cases, the plague is matched by the sorcerers of Egypt (7:22). The form concludes with Pharaoh's response in a renewed hardening of heart (7:23), which sets the stage for the next plague.

Yet there are elements in the story of the first plague that deserve special comment. In 7:15, the site where Moses and Aaron are to confront Pharaoh is specified. They are to meet the king on the bank of the Nile as he goes "out to the water," presumably for his morning bath (compare 8:20). This recalls the rescue of the infant Moses by Pharaoh's daughter who "came down to bathe at the river" (2:5). The rescue of Moses and the beginning effort to deliver Israel share a common geographical orientation. The portrayal of Pharaoh at the river also prepares the reader for the character of the first plague: the transformation of the Nile into blood.

Egyptian art depicting Pharaoh Horemheb

Verse 7:15 also portrays Moses as carrying the staff that had been turned into a snake (the Hebrew word is the same as that used in 4:3, not the "dragon" term of 7:9, etc.). Though Moses' and Aaron's staffs also appear in other parts of the cycle of plague stories (e.g., 8:5), their introduction here is significant. Often rulers in ancient times were depicted carrying symbols of their authority. Even pictures of royal mummy cases from ancient Egypt show the twin symbols of authority clasped in the pharaoh's hands: a shepherd's crook in one hand (presumably representing the pharaoh's guardianship of his people) and a whip in the other (an apparent symbol of the pharaoh's power to punish the wicked). While no detailed description of Moses' or Aaron's staff is given, ancient readers of this text would have understood them to be symbolic of both the authority and the responsibility bestowed by God on Moses.

Free to Worship

Moses' speech from God (7:16) is curious in one important respect. After an initial demand, "Let my people go," a rationale is provided: "so that they may worship me in the wilderness." In the plague narratives, this worship defense is a frequently stated reason for Israel's freedom (8:1, 20, and elsewhere). Notice how the theme develops. In 8:25 Pharaoh says, in effect, that the Israelites are free to worship where they are in Egypt. There is no need to let them go. Moses protests that the Israelites' rituals are so offensive to the Egyptians, they cannot worship in Egypt in safety (8:26–28). Their lives would be endangered. Moses adds that the tribes will journey only a three-day distance to worship their God—a statement that strongly suggests that Mount Horeb/Sinai is the spot in mind. Pharaoh agrees to this request. He even asks for Moses' prayers, only to change his mind (or harden his heart) later (8:28, 32).

Moses continues to insist that the Israelites be freed in order to worship their God (9:13; 10:3). Finally Pharaoh, at the urging of his officials, asks Moses how many people Moses wants to take beyond the borders of Egypt to worship. When Moses replies that all Israelites must go—"our young and our old," "our sons and our daughters and with our flocks and herds" (10:9)—Pharaoh declares such a thing to be unthinkable. Only the men may go because Pharaoh suspects, in his own words, "that you have some evil purpose in mind" (10:10–11).

Want to Know More?

About snakes or serpents? See Paul J. Achtemeier, ed., *Harper's Bible Dictionary* (San Francisco: Harper & Row, 1985), 928–29.

About plagues? See Achtemeier, ed., *Harper's Bible Dictionary*, 801–02; J. Gerald Janzen, *Exodus*, Westminster Bible Companion (Louisville, Ky.: Westminster John Knox Press, 1997), 69–79; Brevard S. Childs, *The Book of Exodus*, Old Testament Library (Philadelphia: Westminster Press, 1974), 130–70.

About hardening Pharaoh's heart? For a thorough discussion, see Terence E. Fretheim, *Exodus*, Interpretation (Louisville, Ky.: John Knox Press, 1991), 96–103; Janzen, *Exodus*, 71–70; Childs, *The Book of Exodus*, 170–75; H. L. Ellison, *Exodus*, Daily Study Bible (Philadelphia: Westminster Press, 1982), 203.

Finally Pharaoh consents to permit the people to leave the country in order to worship, "but your flocks and herds shall remain behind" (10:24). Just as Pharaoh knew earlier that the men would never abandon their wives and children, so now he is shrewd enough to understand that the people would not leave behind their livelihood, their sheep and goats. Moses refuses the offer on the grounds that the livestock were needed for purposes of worship (10:26). Moses is convinced that this is the last conversation he and Pharaoh will ever have! (But note 12:31.)

There is a troubling element in these exchanges. While the people do worship when they reach Mount Horeb/Sinai (Exodus 19), they appear to have no intention of stopping there or of ever returning to Egypt. At this time, no indication is given about traveling on to their ultimate inheritance, the land of Canaan (note Ex. 13:11 and elsewhere). That Moses was not entirely forthcoming with Pharaoh about the larger purposes of the exodus is puzzling. Pharaoh suspected a ruse, the "evil purpose" of 10:10. Was Moses trying to trick Pharaoh, or did Moses actually think of the exodus as a short journey out into the desert? The text is not entirely clear.

The Conversation with Pharaoh

Another interesting feature of the text which is established in the narrative of the first plague is the growing involvement of Pharaoh himself in the conversation with Moses. To trace the trajectories of this involvement requires a bit of repetition, but the subject is significant and deserves to be treated in some detail. In our immediate text (7:14–24) Pharaoh never speaks, but his rejection of Moses' demand for the Israelites' freedom is implied. Not till after the visitation of the second plague (the frogs) is Pharaoh first quoted directly (8:8). It is as if the text is intending to say that since he has two serious catastrophes on his hands, finally Pharaoh will give the matter his attention.

The next time Pharaoh speaks directly, the circumstances are similar. The fourth plague has resulted in an infestation of gnats, so that the king summons Moses and Aaron (as he did in 8:8) and begins to negotiate with them. As noted above, he suggests that if it is freedom to worship that the Israelites are seeking, they have that freedom right here in Egypt. To this Moses replies that they may worship in Egypt only by putting their lives in jeopardy. Although Pharaoh seems to relent (8:25–29), his acquiescence proves short-lived.

A subsequent conversation between Pharaoh and the two Israelite leaders follows the seventh plague (a hailstorm). Again Pharaoh demands that Moses and Aaron appear before him (9:27), and this time the king seems to be the very soul of contrition: "I have sinned; Yahweh is in the right, and I and my people are in the wrong. . . . I will let you go; you need stay no longer" (9:27–28). Someone who read this story for the first time and who did not know its eventual outcome might believe that the Israelites would soon march peacefully out of Egypt. But either Pharaoh is trying to wiggle out of his predicament by extending false promises or he changes his mind. As soon as the storm dissipates, Pharaoh "harden[s] his heart" and decides that the Israelites must stay right where they are (9:34–35).

The next direct conversation involving the Egyptian king results from the threat of another plague (the eighth—locusts). Pharaoh's advisers counsel the king that enough is enough, and that he must let the people go before the land is ruined further (10:7). Again Pharaoh attempts to negotiate a deal with Moses and Aaron, suggesting that only the men go out into the desert to worship their God (10:8–11). That is clearly not what Moses and Aaron are after, so the locusts are visited on all the land of Egypt (10:12–15). Once more Pharaoh seems to repent (10:16–17), but this change of heart is no more authentic than before.

A seemingly final conversation is recorded between Pharaoh and the Israelite leaders preceding the ninth plague. This time, when threatened with darkness over the entire land, Pharaoh orders the Israelites to leave. There is a catch: they must abandon their livestock (10:24). As noted already, Moses will not accept this arrangement. Pharaoh flies into a rage: "Get away from me! Take care that you do not see my face again, for on the day that you see my face you shall die" (10:28). Moses is left with no choice but to comply.

One could draw an interesting psychological profile of Egypt's ruler from these conversations. On the one hand, he is a clever negotiator, who tries to get out of a difficult situation with as little loss to himself and to Egypt as possible. On the other, he is a willful tyrant, blind to the realities of the situation into which he has been thrust. He makes impossible demands on the Israelites until all hope of a peaceful accommodation breaks down. Of course the text is less interested in psychology than in theology. In reality this series of conversations between Pharaoh and the Israelites is another portrait of how puny the power of Pharaoh and of Egypt's gods is when contrasted with that of Yahweh, Israel's God and the Lord of all creation.

So, in our present text, both Pharaoh and the Egyptians are punished for the king's obstinate refusal to comply with Moses' demands. When Moses, under Yahweh's direction, commands Aaron to take staff in hand and extend it over the waters of the Nile, those waters turn to blood. Greek historian Herodotus (fifth century B.C.), referred to Egypt—quite independently of our story—as the "gift of the Nile," because of the absolute reliance of the Egyptian people on the regular flow of the river's water. The story of the first plague has that reliance in mind. The transformation of the water into blood is nothing less than a threat to Egypt's very existence! Had the plague not been lifted after seven days (an event not described in the text, but implied by 7:25), all Egyptians and presumably all Israelites would have perished.

The sorcerers of Egypt match the power of Moses' and Aaron's

God (7:22; 8:7; but compare 8:18; 9:11). What is meant by "the magicians of Egypt did the same by their secret arts" is not clear. The water of the Nile is still blood after the Egyptian sorcerers have performed their magic, so they do not reverse Moses' and Aaron's miracle. The implication is that the Egyptian conjurers turned some other water into blood, since the Nile is the only river in Egypt.

The evidence suggests that 7:22 is a statement not about physics but about theology. The contest between Yahweh and the gods of Egypt is a real contest, not something phony. Pharaoh and all his authoritarian powers of state present themselves as an actual threat to the sovereignty of Israel's God. This being the case, the victory of Yahweh over the armies of the Egyptian king at the Red Sea is a genuine victory (note Ex. 15:1–18).

> "To the modern mind the transformation miracle is incredible, and . . . [it] is further inclined to ask where the water came from for the magicians to operate upon! The ancient narrator probably had no difficulty believing that the water all over Egypt was transformed into blood by Yahweh's power, then transformed back into water, and then into blood again by the Egyptian magicians!" —J. P. Hyatt, *Exodus*, New Century Bible (Grand Rapids: Wm. B. Eerdmans Publishing Co., 1971), 100–101.

In keeping with the manner in which chapters 7–12 portray the pharaoh as one who becomes involved in the conversation with Moses only after the passage of time, the king is described as aloof and disconnected from the plight of his people—a typical character flaw of the world's tyrants. He "turned and went into his house, and he did not take even this to heart" (7:23). Perhaps he had been emboldened by the power of his own sorcerers to match the "wonders" of Moses and Aaron. Childs (154) quotes a Jewish midrash (that is, a commentary) that has Pharaoh tell Moses: "You don't trouble me, for if I can't have water, I'll have wine."

> "This sign was more than just a bloody mess, a lot of dead fish, and a headache for waterworks personnel. It was an ominous sign for Pharaoh, but it didn't sink into his consciousness." —Terence E. Fretheim, *Exodus*, Interpretation, 115–16.

A bitter struggle lies ahead for Moses and Aaron. They may be convinced that Yahweh is on their side and that Israel, by God's strength, will ultimately prevail. But that does not mean that they are only playacting. The power of Pharaoh—the world's most fearsome monarch—and the power of Egypt's gods is genuine and will confront them at every turn. Moses and Aaron are resolute, for they know that the road to freedom lies straight through Pharaoh's court.

Questions for Reflection

1. Part of the rationale for the Israelites to leave Egypt was their need to be free to worship. In fact, as the story of Exodus plays itself out, this foreshadows trouble later on, when the Israelites take liberties with worship (i.e., the golden calf). What are other instances of foreshadowing and irony in this passage?

2. The role of Pharaoh is interesting, among many reasons because it is unclear whether Pharaoh stands against or participates in the plan of God. How do you see Pharaoh standing against the plan of God? Participating in the plan of God?

3. The magicians, through the use of their secret arts, are able to replicate the wonder (plague) in this passage. Maybe Pharaoh was unconvinced of Moses' request because of his own magicians' craft. What might it take to convince you that God wanted you to change your mind?

4. In 7:7 we are told the age of Moses and Aaron. It is a seemingly minor detail, but perhaps it helps set some of the context for the plagues and the coming deliverance of the Israelites. Comparing verse 7 with the preceding verses in Exodus 6, what might telling the age of Moses and Aaron contribute to our understanding of this passage?

4

Free at Last!

The narrative of the first Passover is a pivotal story in the Old Testament from which the Jews have derived great inspiration over the centuries, and in which Christians have found ways to better understand the death of Jesus Christ. The structure of Exodus 12 is straightforward: (1) Yahweh addresses Moses and Aaron about the details of the observance of the first Passover (12:1–20). (2) In response, Moses conveys the instructions to the people, though in a slightly different form (12:21–28). (3) Yahweh kills all the firstborn of Egypt. In response, the Egyptians not only permit the Israelites to leave but virtually compel them to do so (12:29–39). (4) There is a concluding summary (12:40–51).

The Passover is Instituted

Up to this point (12:1), the Egyptians have suffered nine plagues of varying seriousness. Their purpose was to punish Pharaoh for his obstinacy and to provide him with "wonders" or "signs" to convince him that Moses' God is none other than the Lord of creation whose will must be obeyed. Although Pharaoh's

A Passover meal

position has by now softened, he still will not consent to Moses' demands. As 7:23 hints, perhaps that is because none of the plagues has touched Pharaoh personally in any profound way. That is about to change.

Immediately prior to the events of Exodus 12, Moses told the people the precise nature of Yahweh's plans for a tenth and final plague (11:4–8): Yahweh will kill the firstborn of every Egyptian, from the pharaoh himself to the most humble household slave. (Note 12:29, which cites even the prisoners in Egyptian jails as targets.) Not even livestock will be spared, presumably because of their monetary value to the Egyptians. Only the Israelites will be spared, and they will be spared totally. Not even a dog will growl at any Israelite, either any Israelite person or any Israelite beast (11:7)!

Having made these promises, Yahweh sets out to keep them.

First, Yahweh tells the people, through Moses and Aaron, the exact method for sacrificing the passover lamb (12:1–13). Only an unblemished male, one year old, is to be slaughtered, and the body is to be divided into portions of food for the members of each Israelite household. The lamb is to be prepared in a precise manner (roasted, not boiled) and eaten in a precise manner (the people are to be clothed in a particular way—ready for flight, with staffs in their hands). Whatever is uneaten of the lamb shall be consigned to the flames. In the meantime—and this is of utmost importance—the blood of the lamb is to be sprinkled on the two doorposts and the lintel of the entrance to each Israelite home. The reason: "When I [Yahweh] see the blood, I will pass over you, and no plague shall destroy you when I strike the land of Egypt" (12:13).

> **"No leaven shall be found in your houses . . ."** —Exodus 12:19, NRSV
>
> "So important was the removal of leaven that it had to be removed completely before the feast began. . . . Even today in Israel all the leaven in the country is sold to a high Christian cleric, who sells it back once the feast is over." —H. L. Ellison, *Exodus*, Daily Study Bible (Philadelphia: Westminster Press, 1982), 66.

Yahweh's address to Moses and Aaron continues, but the focus moves from the immediate present to all the future years that Israel will exist (12:14–20). In other words, the discussion shifts from the first Passover to all the annual Passover festivals that Israel will observe down through the generations. "This day" (12:14), presumably a reference to the fourteenth day of the first month of the year (by the Jewish calendar the fourteenth of Nisan) (12:6), will be the occasion of the annual Passover celebration in perpetuity. Interestingly, these directions for the future celebrations of Passover make no mention of a Passover lamb, but stress the importance of eating unleavened bread, whose mention is absent from 12:1–20. Many scholars view this dissonance as the historical fusion of two separate festivals, one having to do with the sacrifice of the lamb (perhaps a festival of nomadic herdsmen, such as Moses in his days in the desert of Midian), and the other (perhaps an agricultural, that is Canaanite, festival) tied to the spring harvest. As elsewhere in the Old Testament, this fusion has some literary tension. (Note also Lev. 23:4–15, which combines unleavened bread, the unblemished lamb, and a third element, the first fruits of the harvest, as integral components of the Passover festival.)

Moses Tells the People

Moses addresses the elders of the people about how they are to keep the first Passover (12:21–28). In one sense, these directions are more specific than those delivered by Yahweh (note 12:22), but in another sense they are less specific. There is no mention of how the lamb is to be slaughtered and eaten. Instead, the emphasis is on the presence of the sprinkled blood as a signal to Yahweh that the house is occupied by Israelites. Those who live behind the blood-splattered doorposts will be saved. Some scholars see an older tradition concerning the first Passover in 12:21–28 than that contained in 12:1–13.

> "The [blood] is not simply a 'marker,' as if any colorful substance that caught the eye would do. . . . The blood was the life *of creation* given for the people who lived in the marked houses." —Terence E. Fretheim, *Exodus*, Interpretation, 138.

The Killing of the Firstborn

Verses 29–39 are the most gripping part of chapter 12, at least in terms of dramatic intensity. The promise/threat of 11:4–8 is now realized. At midnight, Yahweh moves through the land, passing over all the Israelite homes. Yahweh enters the home of each Egyptian, from the royal palace to the rankest dungeon—even into the stalls of the animals—and kills every firstborn child or beast.

The reaction of the Egyptians is immediate and agonized. "Pharaoh arose in the night . . . and there was a loud cry in Egypt, for there was not a house without someone dead" (12:30). Now the final (in spite of 10:29) conversation between Moses and Pharaoh occurs. As promised in 6:1, the Israelites are let go, in fact they are chased out of the land. "Go," says Pharaoh. "Take your flocks and your herds . . . and be gone." Pharaoh has seen the light at last. The mightiest potentate on earth now understands that he has been in a contest with one mightier than he, the sovereign of all creation. There is something pitiful in his parting request of Moses: "And bring a blessing on me too!" (12:32).

After relieving their Egyptian neighbors of some of their most valued possessions (note discussion below under "Problems with the Passover Story"), the Israelites depart for the wilderness. The six hundred thousand heads of families are joined by others, an indeterminate "mixed crowd" (12:38), so that the mass of humanity envisioned here must have numbered more than a million.

Summary Comments by the Text

The conclusion (12:40–51) begins with a chronological statement: the Israelites had been in Egypt for 430 years. Then another reminder of the perpetual nature of the Passover celebration is given (12:40–42). Then the summary gives another set of instructions about the annual celebration of the Passover. In this instance, the emphasis is on those persons who are eligible to participate (12:43–50). Finally (12:50–51), the summary ends with a flourish of two sentences stating (1) what the people did and (2) what Yahweh did:

"All the Israelites did just as Yahweh had commanded . . ."
"That very day Yahweh brought the Israelites out of the land of Egypt . . ."

"FREE AT LAST! FREE AT LAST! THANK GOD ALMIGHTY, WE'RE FREE AT LAST!"

For some time scholars believed that the form of the text of 12:1–51 is tied to use in ancient Israel's worship. While they disagree as to details, there is a wide consensus that this passage probably has a liturgical function. This does not deny the historical reality behind the narrative, but calls attention to the application the story received in the life of those people to whom it meant the most. In other words, the text observes that the community of faith cannot take the narrative seriously without responding through the worship of God.

There is evidence that Passover was the central annual worship experience of ancient Israel. Leviticus 23:4–15 and Deuteronomy 16:1–8 enjoin Israel to keep the Passover. Second Chronicles 30:1–27 describes how King Hezekiah reinstituted the Passover after a period of non-observance; 2 Kings 23:21–23 tells a similar story from the time of King Josiah. (In both passages, Passover is an event consigned to the Jerusalem Temple and organized by the king and the priests in a highly centralized manner, while in Exodus 12, as in modern Jewish practice, Passover is a celebration centered largely in the home.) So even though neglected from time to time, Passover was at the heart of ancient Israel's life before God.

> "Our outward ritual of worship should be calculated to arouse our children's curiosity." —H. L. Ellison, *Exodus*, Daily Study Bible (Philadelphia: Westminster Press, 1982), 67.

There are many who believe that Exodus 12, particularly 12:1–27 and 12:43–49, was tied to those moments when Israel remembered God's miraculous involvement in history, and celebrated the new life that the nation received both *then* and *now*. Exodus 12, then, is an example of layering of faith history and worship material. For ancient Israel (and modern Jews), Passover is both a historical truth and a contemporary proclamation!

God's Contemporary Actions

This brings us to an element in the Old Testament which might be called the "eternal contemporaneity" of events narrated in the

Structure of Exodus 12:1-15:21

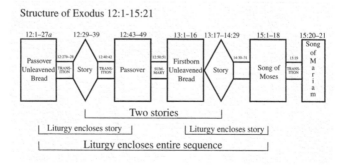

Two versions of the Passover story are layered in with liturgical material in Exodus 12ff. (From Terence E. Fretheim, *Exodus*, Interpretation, 134.)

biblical text. This concept is stated most graphically in Deuteronomy about the Mount Horeb/Sinai experience, when Israel received the Ten Commandments from Yahweh. In spite of forty years in the wilderness and the occurrence of many births and deaths among the Israelites, Moses declares:

> Yahweh our God made a covenant with us at Horeb. Not with our ancestors did Yahweh make this covenant, but with us, who are all of us here alive today. (Deut. 5:2–3)

That which modern readers think of as "Old Testament history" is not considered history by the text itself, but instead as living proclamation. That is no truer of anything in the Old Testament than the event of the Passover. Each time Israel celebrated this exciting festival, it relived the experience of Moses and of Moses' contemporaries, and claimed their freedom as its own. In much the same manner, the resurrection of Christ is renewed each year at Easter—and indeed every Sunday of the year, the weekly resurrection festival for Christians.

As some commentators have pointed out, this understanding of the text helps explain the enormous numbers cited in Exodus 12:37–38. These figures perhaps represent the approximate population of the nation during the reign of King Solomon, and are another means by which the Passover experience is appropriated by later generations of faithful Israelites (see Fretheim, 144). The question in the wonderful spiritual, "Were you there when they crucified my Lord?" might be paraphrased, "Were you there when they slaughtered the passover lamb?" As noted below, Passover and Good Friday have many things in common, not the least of which is the way in which a past event is made into one that also takes place in the present and the future.

"[This is] an attempt to make past present, to teach through a repetition that aims to create experience rather than simply transmit information." —John I. Durham, *Exodus*, Word Biblical Commentary, 163.

Problems with the Passover Story

For all the glorious exuberance, however, the story of the first Passover contains some troubling features, two in particular: the

Israelites' acquisition of the possessions of their Egyptian captors and the death of Egypt's firstborn.

The First Problem

The first issue is raised initially in Exodus 3:21–22. There, when Yahweh inaugurates a call to Moses, the promise is made that Israel will be freed from Egyptian bondage, and that the Egyptians will pay a price in "jewelry of silver and gold, and clothing." In other words, Israel "shall plunder the Egyptians" (note also 11:2). In 12:35–36 that promise comes true, being described in words that closely parallel 3:21–22. Now, one might have some empathy if the Israelite slaves believed that the Egyptians owed them compensation for all the painful years when they toiled for little or no reward. But should God have joined in the quest for reparations? On what ethical basis would Yahweh have justified a role in the despoiling of the Egyptians?

> **Beware the leaven**
>
> Old habits die hard. Though the Israelites may have left all of their leavened *bread* in Egypt, their later use of the silver and gold, which they did take, betrays that they didn't leave behind all the "leaven" that was hidden within them. —See J. Gerald Janzen, *Exodus*, Westminster Bible Companion, 84.

Two features of the text soften the moral issues involved. First, the Egyptians seem to have given of their treasures willingly (note 3:22). Second, as Childs points out (176), the verb translated "asked" in 12:35 may also be translated "borrow" (although surely no one seriously thought that the Israelites would return their "plunder"). To many, especially those who themselves or whose ancestors have been subjected to forced labor, the idea of reparations seems only just. But to others, this feature of the text is an embarrassment. God seems portrayed as involved in a deceptive and unethical act.

The Second Problem

This dilemma pales in comparison with that presented by Yahweh's slaughter of all of Egypt's firstborn. Earlier, the text described very negatively (1:15–22) how an earlier pharaoh had condemned to death all the Israelite baby boys. (Although, in fairness, it should be noted that not a single death is reported!) Perhaps even more to the point, the Gospel of Matthew condemns wicked King Herod for his murder of Jewish children at the time of the birth of Jesus (Matt.

2:16–18). The really terrifying question is: Is Yahweh's slaughter of the Egyptian firstborn substantially different from Herod's murder of the Jewish innocents? To be sure, one may point out that God's purposes and Herod's were fundamentally different. God was about the business of freeing an oppressed people. Herod, in the fashion of a paranoid, was attempting to defend his tottering throne from a supposed enemy.

> "The idea that God destroys his enemies using the powers of nature is a part of the common theology of the ancient Near East that Israel shared with its neighbors." — Donald E. Gowan, *Theology in Exodus: Biblical Theology in the Form of a Commentary* (Louisville, Ky.: Westminster John Knox Press, 1994), 147.

Did God really have to kill all those firstborn to get the point across to Pharaoh, including the death of the child of the enslaved woman grinding grain (Ex. 11:5) and the child of the prisoner in the dungeon (12:29), who themselves may have been as brutalized by Pharaoh as any Israelite? In other words, is Yahweh guilty of murder here? Or manslaughter?

Suggestions for Solutions

These are tough questions—in a sense, unanswerable questions. These questions are more easily asked and answered by someone who is sitting in a comfortable room writing or reading this book, someone whose life has been unscarred by oppression from the hand of others. How much different would the questions—and their answers—seem to one in the terrible jaws of oppression? Like the potential victim of a drowning who flails at the water in the search for any gulp of air, the oppressed must understandably regard any effort to gain their freedom as a wonderful end in itself, regardless of the means. So what if a few hundred thousand Egyptians die at the hands of God in order that Israel might be free? A small price to pay, one might think. Besides, consider the indescribable suffering of the innumerable victims of Egyptian persecution!

"But this is God," the person in the easy chair responds. "The victim of oppression may rejoice at the despoiling of the Egyptians and at their loss of life. But God is the God of the Egyptians, as well as of the Israelites. Shouldn't Yahweh be held to a higher standard?"

Two considerations, while not solving a troubling dilemma, may at least help. The first is: the Old Testament takes evil very seriously. Evil has corrupted human life and destroyed much human happiness (Genesis 2–3), and it is evil that has interposed itself between what would otherwise be a harmonious relationship between God and humankind. Because of the corrosive effect of evil, God stands in judgment on evil in all its forms (note, as one of many examples from prophetic literature, Jer. 7:8–15). God repudiates evil and seeks to destroy it root and branch. Men and women of faith, who trust God and who are themselves committed to the repudiation of evil, would not want it any other way.

A second consideration is that, like many of their neighbors in the ancient world, the Hebrews of old made little if any distinction between evil as an abstraction and persons who do evil deeds. For example, Satan is mentioned infrequently in the Old Testament, and there is little discussion, as there is with most modern women and men, as to any difference between an evil deed and and an overarching evil force (or mental condition) that caused the deed. It is quite normative in the world of the Old Testament to equate evil actions with the persons who perform them. (If this seems to be an outdated ethical problem, we may remember that almost every jury in a criminal trial in our own time must ask itself the question, Is this person actually responsible for the crime which he/she has committed, or were they driven to it by forces over which they had no control?) Seen in this light, the narratives in Exodus consider the Israelites' enslavement to be the evil activity of the Egyptians, not just of Pharaoh. They further consider that an appropriate means for God to deal with this evil is to attack those persons who represent it. So the death of the Egyptian children is not as problematic an issue for those who first wrote and read Exodus 12 as it may be for you and me.

Passover and Christ's Sacrifice

As noted above, Passover is important for Christians because it offers an interpretative paradigm of the death of Jesus. The four Gospels are unanimous in pointing out the relationship between the Old Testament Passover and the sacrifice of Christ on the cross, even as they approach the connection from somewhat different perspectives (the Synoptic Gospels—Matthew, Mark, and Luke—portray the Last Supper as a Passover meal, while John emphasizes Jesus' role as the Passover Lamb). Although the Gospels are among the last parts of the New Testament to have been written, they unquestionably reflect an identification between the sacrifice of the Passover lamb and the death of Christ that was made by the very first Christians, who were also Jews.

In addition to the narrative of the death of Jesus, at least three other New Testament texts deserve mention. (1) In Mark 8:27–33 (paralleled by Matt. 16:13–23 and Luke 9:18–22), a watershed moment is reached in the relationship between Jesus and his disciples when Peter, as the spokesman for the group, confesses that Jesus is the long-awaited Christ, or Messiah, sent by God. To the surprise of his friends, Jesus immediately begins to speak in a manner quite different from that which the disciples expect of the Messiah. He begins to describe his suffering and death. Quite clearly this passage makes a firm connection between the role of the Messiah in God's redemptive activity and that of the Suffering Servant of Isaiah 52:13–53:12 (and Isaiah's description sounds very like a Passover lamb!).

At the Last Supper, Jesus gave a new meaning to the Passover meal.

Peter's revulsion over the linking of these two personalities (Mark 8:32) reflects the distance between the disciples' understanding of messiahship and that of Jesus. But the Matthew passage also makes clear that in Jesus' death and resurrection, the ultimate meaning of Jesus' life is to be found, as well the ultimate hope for a sinful humanity.

(2) In 1 Corinthians 5:7–8, Paul clearly has the Jewish Passover in mind:

> Clean out the old yeast so that you may be a new batch, as you really are unleavened. For our paschal [passover] lamb, Christ, has been sacrificed. Therefore, let us celebrate the festival, not with the old yeast, the yeast of malice and evil, but with the unleavened bread of sincerity and truth.

What is striking here is not only that the death of Christ is identified with the death of the Passover lamb, but the church is identified as the New Israel, rejecting the leaven of sin and embracing the unleavened bread of faithfulness to God and purity in the manner of their lives.

(3) In 1 Peter 1:17–21 there is another clear reference to the Jewish Passover. The passage begins by admitting that though the people are still living "in exile" (in a sinful and cruel world), they should know that they have already been ransomed. How? Not by the usual means of ransom, silver and gold, but "with the precious blood of Christ, like that of a lamb without defect or blemish." The role of Jesus as the Passover Lamb has been determined from all eternity, the text goes on to say, but has only just been revealed, in order that the church may "trust in God, who raised him from the dead and gave him glory, so that your faith and hope are set on God." The sacrifice of Christ is described as the fulfillment of the Passover of old, as the means by which the power of God is made clearly evident and also the means by which faithful people are transformed from a state of despair to one of hope.

(Be aware that the theological "flow" of these ideas was probably the reverse of that stated above. Instead of the concept of the Messiah as Suffering Servant giving rise to that of the Messiah as Passover Lamb, the opposite may have occurred in the life of the early church. The answer to this question lies in the much-debated issue of which sayings attributed to the "historical Jesus" actually came from his lips, and which are the contributions of an infant church.)

It is thus no exaggeration to say that Exodus 12:51, with its exuberant declaration of freedom, is to be understood as a political statement only to a limited extent. In reality, Exodus 12:51 is a statement about the human condition before God—namely, that the God who brought order out of chaos (Gen. 1:1) and who presides

Want to Know More?

About Passover? For the history of Passover, see Werner H. Schmidt, *The Faith of the Old Testament: A History* (Philadelphia: Westminster Press, 1983), 119–23. For how Passover is observed today, see Celia Brewer Marshall, *A Guide through the Old Testament* (Louisville, Ky.: Westminster John Knox Press, 1989), 45–46.

About the destroyer? See George Arthur Buttrick, ed., *The Interpreter's Dictionary of the Bible*, vol. 1 (Nashville: Abingdon Press, 1962), 830. For a discussion of the angel of Yahweh, see Horst Dietrich Preuss, *Old Testament Theology*, vol. 1, Old Testament Library (Louisville, Ky.: Westminster John Knox Press, 1995), 165–66. For a thorough discussion of the Divine Destroyer, see Donald E. Gowan, *Theology in Exodus: Biblical Theology in the Form of a Commentary* (Louisville, Ky.: Westminster John Knox Press, 1994), 127–67.

About the plunder of the Egyptians? See John Van Seters, *The Life of Moses: The Yahwist as Historian in Exodus–Numbers* (Louisville, Ky.: Westminster John Knox Press, 1994), 97–99; Brevard S. Childs, *The Book of Exodus*, Old Testament Library (Philadelphia: Westminster Press, in compassionate sovereignty over creation is also the one who redeems women and men from evil in all its forms. The first Passover anticipates a newly constituted and reclaimed Israel. The Passover death of Christ anticipates new life for all who respond to its power and love, and who give themselves in faith to the Passover Lamb.

"THANK GOD ALMIGHTY, WE'RE FREE AT LAST!"

? Questions for Reflection

1. Passover is both an annual celebration and a remembrance of a significant event in history. What days are set aside to celebrate and remember significant events in history (either in secular history or the history of the church)? Why do we celebrate those days? Part of the celebration of Passover includes a reading or retelling of the Passover story. What are some of the stories we tell about the history of our faith?

2. As with some of the earlier stories in Exodus, the Passover story presents some tensions with how we understand events today, either scientifically or theologically. Along with earlier tensions (like God hardening hearts, Moses lying to Pharaoh, etc.), how do you reconcile the killing of the firstborn?

3. Mention has been made in this unit of a connection between Passover and the portrayal of the passion of Jesus in John's Gospel. Using what you know of Passover and the passion of Jesus in John, what are some of those connections?

4. The Passover observance is explained in verses 26–27 as a means to answer a question, "Why do we have this observance?" In the Christian tradition, the Lord's Supper stems from a Passover meal. What are some similarities between the Lord's Supper and the Jewish Passover meal? When children ask about the Lord's Supper, "Why do we have this observance?" what would be a good response?

Exodus 14:1–31 **5**

The Miracle at the Red Sea

As noted earlier (unit 3), though the stories about the ten plagues are a prominent feature of the book of Exodus (Exodus 7–12), these stories receive little attention in the rest of the Bible. But the narrative of the miraculous crossing of the Red Sea is one of the most celebrated acts of God, as far as the Old Testament is concerned. Moreover, just as the Passover celebration is viewed in the New Testament as a paradigm for the sacrificial death of Christ (see unit 4), so the miracle at the Red Sea becomes a model of Christ's resurrection for early Christians. The narratives of the first Passover and of the Red Sea deliverance are similar to the stories of Christ's death and resurrection in the New Testament, in that the second story of each pair is meaningless without the first.

The Red Sea

Background to the Crossing

The story of the Red Sea miracle begins in 13:17–22 with an explanation for the Israelites' circuitous route from Egypt into Palestine, their final destination. That explanation, "if the people face war [from the Philistines and others in southern Palestine], they may

49

change their minds and return to Egypt" (13:17), speaks to the Israelites' precarious state of mind. During the long negotiations between Moses and Pharaoh, the Israelites were silent. The events that lie ahead will test their trust in either Moses or Moses' God. This is

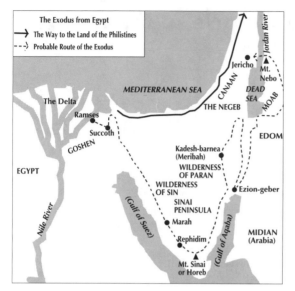

the first warning that the people whom Moses leads are often weak and fickle. Though they go out "prepared for battle" (v. 18), there is actually not much fight in them. Verse 17 also explains geographically why the Israelites exit Egypt in the direction of the Sinai desert instead into the Negev. The direct route led east, but now the Israelites find themselves near the Red Sea.

A second feature of 13:17–22 is the reference to the bones of Joseph in 13:19. This statement recalls the end of Genesis (Gen. 50:24–26) and serves as a reminder that the amazing story of Israel's life in Egypt, begun with the story of Joseph (Genesis 37ff.), is now over.

A third and final feature is the description of Yahweh's presence as a pillar of cloud by day and of fire by night (13:21–22). This is the first of many references where Yahweh provides affirmation and guidance to the people during the journey ahead (note 14:19–20 and elsewhere).

With Their Backs to the Sea

The background is given, and now the characters set the stage for a miracle. In verses 1–4, Yahweh tells Moses to position the people between Pharaoh's armies and the water, with their backs to the Red Sea. An ever-watchful Pharaoh interprets this apparently senseless maneuver as aimless wandering. When Yahweh hardens Pharaoh's heart, Pharaoh jumps at the opportunity to spring the trap into which Israel seemingly has stumbled. But Pharaoh's intentions are at cross-purposes with those of Yahweh, and as it plays out, it is the Egyptian king who stumbles into a trap. Yahweh states the purpose: "I will gain glory for myself . . . and the Egyptians shall know that I am Yahweh" (v. 4).

> "[Yahweh] sets a puzzling route no [one] would have thought of, to confuse Pharaoh by an appearance of confusion and to win further and final glory himself at Pharaoh's expense." —John I. Durham, *Exodus, Word Biblical Commentary*, 187.

Verses 5–9 describe Pharaoh's pursuit of the Israelites in some detail. Mentioning chariots in the Egyptian army, including Pharaoh's personal chariot (v. 6), is in keeping with the historical record. The armies of the Pharaohs were among the most skilled in the ancient world in using this device of speed and power. Six hundred chariots represents a large force, and perhaps reflects the number of Israelite fugitives given in 12:37–38.

The dramatic tension of the narrative is heightened in verses 10–14, with the sinister opening phrase, "as Pharaoh drew near . . ." As they would on many occasions when danger threatened, the Israelites turn on Moses in anger. "Weren't there enough graves in Egypt?" they taunt. "Why did you bring us out here to die in the desert? Don't you remember that we told you at the time that we would rather be slaves of Pharaoh than to come out here to die?"

A model of an ancient chariot

(14:11–12, paraphrased). Nowhere have we read previously that the Israelites preferred slavery to a chance for freedom. This seems to be an after-the-fact memory, an "I-told-you-so" attitude so strident as to conjure up a conversation that never took place. At least it is not one which was recorded.

> "God had . . . set them free from what had long held them in bondage. But they, as any of us might, began longing for the devil they knew, rather than face the unknown road ahead." —Kathleen Norris, *Amazing Grace: A Vocabulary of Faith* (New York: Riverhead Books, 1998), 20.

Moses' response to the people is the essence of quiet trust in God. There are at least five elements in this remarkable but brief address to the people (see Fretheim, 156–158):

1. "Don't be afraid." A frequent declaration by God in significant moments in Israel's life (note, for example, Isa. 41:10, 13, 14 and elsewhere).
2. "Stand firm." Meaning that they must trust God to save them.
3. "Keep still." They are not to be passive but are to allow God's will to unfold.
4. "See God's deliverance." Israel is not to be the doer of the great wonder that is about to take place, but is to be a witness to what Yahweh will do.
5. "Yahweh will fight for you." Israel cannot cause this great miracle to occur, but is to be the beneficiary of it, nonetheless.

Verses 15–18 are an address to Moses by Yahweh giving Moses directions for his role in the upcoming deliverance. "Why do you cry out to me?" is directed not at Moses but at the people and their lack of resolve. Moses is to stretch out his hand, containing the staff, and the sea will be divided. Once more Yahweh gives the reason for what is about to occur: ". . . so I will gain glory for myself . . . and the Egyptians will know that I am Yahweh" (v. 18; note v. 4).

Pharaoh's Army Is Swallowed

The stage is set, and the climax to this gripping narrative is reached in verses 19–29, which may be divided into three subsections:

1. Verses 19–20, which describe the positioning of the pillar of cloud/fire.
2. Verses 21–25, which tell of the separating of the waters and the entrapment of the Egyptians.
3. Verses 26–29, which relate the Egyptians' death and the Israelites' deliverance.

Verses 19–20

The pillar of cloud (by day) and of fire (by night) moves between the Israelites and the advancing Egyptian chariots. Cloud is first and then fire, strengthening the understanding that it is twilight, which in the ancient Hebrew reckoning was the end of an old day (in this case, the day of slavery) and the beginning of a new day (a day of freedom).

Verses 21–25

As Moses was directed to do by God (14:16), he stretches out his hand over the waters. Yahweh responds by sending "a strong east wind all night," which splits the sea so that the Israelites can walk across on the sea floor. This means salvation for the Israelites, but entrapment for the Egyptians. Verse 25 graphically describes how the Egyptian chariots become immobilized. Apparently the crossing took all night, for what began at twilight becomes the "morning watch" as Yahweh clogs the wheels of the Egyptian chariots, and "dawn" as the sea returns to its bed (14:27). In Fretheim's telling words (160), "As the morning breaks for Israel, the night falls on the Egyptians." The last sentence of this subsection fulfills the promise of 14:4 and 18. Pharaoh's soldiers cry out, "Let us flee from the Israelites, for Yahweh is fighting for them against Egypt" (v. 25).

Two related topics are often raised in connection with this miraculous event. The first has to do with the nature of the miracle. Because of the reference to the "east wind," many attempt to identify specific natural causes behind the parting of the waters. References to various climatic features of modern Egypt, as well as efforts to identify areas of the Red Sea that are especially shallow and susceptible to a driving back of the waters are cited. Experience has demonstrated, however, that efforts to rationalize this or any other biblical miracle are doomed because the text understands the parting of the waters of the Red Sea *as a miracle.* Judaism is based on a miracle—this one—just as Christianity is based on a miracle—the open tomb. Neither of these great faiths can be deprived of their miraculous element and remain the same.

> "Not tides, not storms, not bad planning, not tactical error, not bad luck, or good luck, but *Yahweh.*" —John I. Durham, *Exodus,* Word Biblical Commentary, 187.

The second topic is the location of the body of water. The Hebrew text refers to the "Reed Sea" or "Sea of Reeds" (*Yam Suph*). This identification has fueled an effort to locate the miraculous crossing in a marshy area of the Nile Delta, in order to support a naturalistic explanation for the miracle. Yet it seems clear that the body of water intended by the writer(s) of this text is the Red Sea, in that it, more than any lake, swamp or stream in the region between Egypt and Sinai, would match the dimensions described in 15:21–29. And so the NRSV and other English versions are correct in their translation (Ex. 13:18; 15:4, 22).

Verses 26–29

This passage is the climax for all of chapter 14. Just as Moses had stretched out his hand at sunset to divide the waters, so now at sunrise he repeats the gesture "and at dawn the sea returned to its normal depth" (v. 27). The awesome phrase "Yahweh tossed the Egyptians into the sea" (v. 27) leaves no doubt that the contest that began with Moses' first appearance before Pharaoh in 7:14–24 has now reached a conclusion. Yahweh has prevailed, not just over Pharaoh (who is not listed among the Egyptian casualties) but also over Egypt's gods.

The miracle at the Red Sea also has cosmological overtones. The sea is prominent in many ancient creation stories, not only the Bible, but also in creation stories of ancient Israel's neighbors. Not surprisingly, there are echoes of Genesis 1 in Exodus 14. The "strong east wind" of Exodus 14:21 uses the same Hebrew noun (*ruach*) as that in Genesis 1:2: "And the Spirit [*ruach*] of God was moving over the face of the waters" (RSV; compare NRSV's less apt translation "while a wind [*ruach*] from God swept over the face of the waters"). In addition, Exodus 14:21 describes the waters as "divided" so that the Israelites might march over on dry land. Genesis 1:6 describes the separation of the waters, those above from those below (compare Gen. 1:9). There can be no question that the text of Exodus 14 intends the readers to understand that Yahweh, the God of Israel, is the creator of the heaven and earth, and that all other gods are no gods at all. As discussed above, the crossing at the Red Sea is portrayed as nothing less than a miracle of God.

> "But this is not presented as a mythological creation struggle between Yahweh and the sea. God wages this fight against the gods of Egypt, and their human representative, Pharaoh." —J. P. Hyatt, *Exodus*, New Century Bible (Grand Rapids: Wm. B. Eerdmans Publishing Co., 1971), 156.

Verses 30–31 provide a concluding summary of the Red Sea narrative. Notice the verbs:

Yahweh saved . . .
Israel saw . . .
Israel saw . . .
The people feared and believed . . .

In the briefest possible way, these verbs define what happened in the incident at the Red Sea.

Records of the Red Sea Elsewhere

As noted, no event in the Old Testament is more celebrated in other parts of the Bible. To discover the evidence, one need go no farther than the next chapter of the book of Exodus. Wide agreement exists among scholars that Exodus 15:1–18 is a song composed in celebration of the Red Sea miracle. Here, a prose account of, and a poetic reflection upon, the same event

> "The verb is *hoshia'* (associated with the proper name *yehoshua'*, Joshua, in Aramaic, *yeshua'*, 'Jesus'), meaning 'deliver, save.'" —J. Gerald Janzen, *Exodus*, Westminster Bible Companion, 102–3).

are side by side in the text. The kernel of the poem, 15:21, is probably older than the prose narrative of chapter 14, and may be among the oldest literary fragments in the Bible:

> Sing to Yahweh, for he has triumphed gloriously;
> horse and rider he has thrown into the sea.

Verses 1–18 repeat (15:1) and expand upon this basic theme to suggest that the normal narrative methods of human communication (Exodus 14) are simply not sufficient to communicate the full and joyous impact of the Red Sea miracle.

The Red Sea episode lived on in Israel's collective memory as did few other experiences, and it was repeatedly rehearsed in song and story. Note, for example, Psalms 77:16–20 and 136:10–15. In addition, many centuries after the time of Moses, an

> "The route so fatal to the Egyptians was a route of deliverance for Israel." —John I. Durham, *Exodus*, Word Biblical Commentary, 196.

anonymous prophet living among the Jewish captives in Babylon who wished to identify a model for the great work of salvation which God was about to work in the lives of the exiles in Babylon, chose the story of God's great deed of salvation in the time of the exiles of Moses' generation:

> I am Yahweh, your Holy One,
> the Creator of Israel, your King.
> Thus says Yahweh,

who makes a way in the sea,
a path in the mighty waters,
who brings out chariot and horse,
army and warrior;
they lie down, they cannot rise,
they are extinguished, quenched like a wick. . . .

I am about to do a new thing;
now it springs forth, do you not perceive it?
I will make a way in the wilderness
and rivers in the desert. . . .

to give drink to . . . the people whom I formed for myself
so that they might declare my praise. (Isa. 43:15–21)

During the last few centuries before the birth of Christ, several Jewish writers addressed themselves to the exodus story, often revealing a great attraction to the event at the Red Sea. One of the more interesting is an Ezekiel who lived in the Mediterranean world (perhaps Alexandria, Egypt) about the second century B.C. This Ezekiel (not the same as the Old Testament prophet of that name) wrote in Greek and was apparently fascinated with ancient Greek culture, especially its literary traditions. Borrowing the style of the great Athenian tragedians of the fifth century B.C. (such dramatists as Aeschylus, Sophocles, and Euripides), he wrote a lengthy play on the theme of Moses and the exodus. Only fragments have survived to the present. It bore the simple title *Exagoge*, meaning "Exodus," and its eyewitness treatment of the miracle at the Red Sea strongly suggests that the play was intended for the stage. (In the days before Hollywood, "staging" a flood would have been a near impossibility!) If *Exagoge* was ever produced theatrically, a likely time would have been at Passover.

The character who describes the Red Sea event is a surviving member of Pharaoh's army, who expresses the matter in this way (notice that some liberties are taken with the biblical text, but the account is clearly drawn from Ex. 14:21–29):

From heaven, then, a shining light like fire
appeared to us, so we were led to think
that God was their defense. For when they reached
the farther shore a mighty wave gushed forth
hard by us, so that one in terror cried,

"Flee back before the hands of the Most High;
to them he offers succor, but to us,
most wretched men, destruction he does work."
The sea-path flooded, all our host was lost. (Charlesworth, 803–19)

Jewish writers' deep interest in the miracle at the Red Sea carried over to the New Testament. As might be expected, the New Testament writers filter the Red Sea story through the church's belief that God's ultimate miracle of deliverance is found in the death and resurrection of Christ. So the connection is made between the Red Sea event and the Christ event. Occasionally, this identification is formalistic and wooden. For example, the Gospel of Matthew describes the return of the holy family from their flight to Egypt by quoting a reference to the exodus by the prophet Hosea (11:1): "Out of Egypt I have called my son" (Matt. 2:15).

Other New Testament writers refer to the exodus, with its crowning moment at the Red Sea, both to celebrate it and to point to its inadequacy. The sermon of Paul in the synagogue at Antioch, quoted in Acts 13:16–41, is a good example of the exodus theme. Verses 13–22 review the history of Israel, emphasizing the exodus from Egypt and God's gift to Israel of the monarchy—in other words, Moses and David. Verse 23 is a transition statement that links the line of David with Israel's true savior, Jesus, and from that point on Paul tells the story of Jesus' life, death, and resurrection. He concludes (vv. 36–41) by comparing the fullness of God's redemptive work in Christ with the incompleteness of that achieved through David and Moses. As for David, he died and "experienced corruption," whereas "he whom God raised up experienced no corruption." As for Moses, he pointed the way to freedom, but full freedom can be achieved only in Christ: "by this Jesus everyone who believes is set free from all those sins from which you could not be freed by the law of Moses."

A similar chord is struck in 1 Corinthians. 10:1–13. There the Red Sea incident is described as a baptism "into Moses" which united the people before God. Even then, the source of their strength was Christ, "the rock that followed them." Yet the people were not faithful to God and were "struck down in the wilderness," an apparent reference to an understanding that the Israelites who reached the Land of Promise were not the same Israelites who left Egypt. Their sins were several: idolatry, sexual immorality, complaints against God. Those who are in Christ, "on whom the ends of the ages have come," must not follow this negative example, but instead rely on God, "who will not let you be tested beyond your strength." (See Childs's discussion of the Red Sea theme in the New Testament, 232–34.)

Some Reflections

Seeing the text of Exodus 14 and the way the Red Sea miracle has been understood allows for several observations: First, few stories in the literature of any people anywhere so wonderfully relate the thrill of freedom newly achieved. This is especially true when one takes into consideration not just the prose account in Exodus 14 but also the rhapsodic poetry of Exodus 15 and its joyous delirium. Only those who have been caged, either literally or figuratively, can resonate to the ecstasy that bursts forth when the cage doors open. It is little wonder that captives—from the Jewish exiles in Babylon in the sixth century B.C. through African American slaves in the eighteenth and nineteenth centuries A.D. to black South Africans in the twentieth century—have used the symbolism of the Red Sea waters-held-at-bay to express their own longings for liberty. In fact, the story of the exodus, and especially that of Exodus 14, has been a recognizable force that has contributed to the breaking of chains that have held people captive.

Second, as potent a symbol as the Red Sea story may be in political and social terms, it is basically a statement about God. As noted above, the contest between Moses and Pharaoh is actually a contest between Yahweh, the God of Israel and the Sovereign of all creation, and every false god or ideology. From the moment that Aaron's staff-turned-dragon devours the staffs-turned-dragons belonging to the priest-magicians of Egypt (Ex. 7:12), it is clear that the struggle at hand is one of cosmological import. It is clear, as well, that Yahweh will prevail. In keeping with this understanding, the language by which the miracle at the Red Sea is conveyed echoes Israel's creation poem in Genesis 1. When Israel becomes a new nation, the emphasis will be upon a nation chosen by God, constituted by God, and maintained by God. So, in spite of its multifaceted implications, Exodus 14 is not a political manifesto or

> "The objective is to bring the Egyptians, indeed the entire world, to the point of knowing that *Israel's* God is the Lord of all the earth." —Terence E. Fretheim, *Exodus*, Interpretation, 154.

a documentation of social upheaval. It is a statement of theology, through and through.

Third, it is clear from the interest the Red Sea miracle has aroused in Christians that the theology of Exodus 14 is a statement to the church and to individual Christians about the freedom that God has won for us from those forces over which we have little or no control: sin, disease, loneliness, pain, and death. The startling statement that Paul makes in 1 Corinthians 10:4 that the real liberator of Pharaoh's slaves was Christ is not due to a slip of the pen, or to a misunderstanding concerning chronology, or a romanticized view of life. Paul declares that the miracle at the Red Sea was a prelude to the miracle of the open tomb, and that the God who raised Jesus from the dead is the same God who held the waters at bay for the Israelites. Even if the freedom won by God at the Red Sea was incomplete, and the original recipients of this gift were not fully responsive, that does not diminish its power. Just as the Red Sea waters become emblematic of Christian baptism, so the miracle at the Red Sea points to the continuing miracle of God's redemptive love in Jesus Christ, a love that continues to work its wonder.

A fourth and final observation concerns the problem of how a Christian can understand the ultimacy of God's revelation in Christ without concluding that, because the Old Testament story anticipates the New Testament story, Judaism is somehow "inferior" to Christianity. That is only a half-step away from the horribly wrongheaded conclusion that Jews (or Muslims, Bud-

 Want to Know More?

About the Red/Reed Sea? See George Arthur Buttrick, ed., *The Interpreter's Dictionary of the Bible,* vol. 4 (Nashville: Abingdon Press, 1962), 19–21.

About spirit, breath, or *ruach*? See Shirley C. Guthrie, *Christian Doctrine,* revised ed. (Louisville, Ky.: Westminster John Knox Press, 1994), 291–313; G. Kittel and G. Friedrich, eds., *Theological Dictionary of the New Testament,* abridged in one volume by Geoffrey W. Bromiley (Grand Rapids: Wm. B. Eerdmans Publishing Co., 1985), 876–84.

dhists, and others) are "inferior" to Christians, a perversion that has led to more injustices in the twentieth century than one cares to think about.

So how does one embrace Acts 13 or 1 Corinthians 10 without becoming anti-Semitic, or even triumphalist? The answer lies in recognizing the strong commonalities and interdependencies between Old and New Testaments, and thus between Judaism and Christianity. It may be that from a Christian perspective, the last word on freedom from sin has been delivered not by Moses but by Christ. Yet it must be admitted that apart from the Old Testament, Christians would have no conceptual basis for even understanding what sin is, in the first place, to say nothing of what it means to be in the hands of a gracious God. In other words, the New Testament has not "trumped" the Old. Rather, the two Testaments, and therefore Judaism and Christianity, are in continuing dialogue with one another, mutually instructing and clarifying the human understanding of God's will for our lives. That is certainly true of the relation between Exodus 14 and its New Testament responses, and it is equally true of the relations between Jews and Christians generally. Not one of us, Jew or Christian, fully lives up to the teaching of either Moses or Christ, and until we do, we are under God's imperative to live gently with all people.

> So, whether you eat or drink, or whatever you do, do everything for the glory of God. Give no offense to Jews or to Greeks or to the church of God. (1 Cor. 10:32)

? Questions for Reflection

1. An abiding feature of this story is the presence of God with the Israelites, calling to mind the portrayal of Jesus as Emmanuel (God with us) in Matthew's Gospel. What are some of the expressions of God's presence in this story? What assistance does this story of God's presence offer you?

2. The Israelites complain to Moses about leaving Egypt. In fact, while they are complaining, God is about to deliver them. Moses gave the Israelites five affirmations just before the miracle of the Red Sea. What are those affirmations? What are ways those affirmations can speak to us today?

3. The strong images of *ruach* (wind or spirit) and water reverberate throughout this story. The story of Jesus' baptism involves water and spirit as well. What are ways baptism is like the Red Sea miracle?

4. This passage looks at a memorable and mighty deed of deliverance. What are other stories from the Bible that speak about deliverance?

Thunder and Lightning, Fire and Smoke: God Appears at Sinai

Exodus 19 is a difficult chapter in Exodus, at least in terms of the challenges presented to the reader who wishes to follow the flow of the narrative. The text displays baffling incongruities and dissonances that are not easily explained, even if one assumes that many hands may have contributed to the shape of the text. For example, in an unbelievable description, Moses seems to scamper up and down the mountain. In verse 3 Moses "went up" the mountain, only to come down again in verse 7. In verse 9 he seems to be back atop the mountain (although the text doesn't explicitly say), while in verse 14 he "went down." In verse 20 Yahweh calls Moses back up the mountain, and in verse 24 orders him down again, but only that he may "come up bringing Aaron with you." Modern tourists who trek up Jebel Musa, a traditional site of the events of Exodus 19, can sympathize with poor Moses. The ascent is so difficult that often a climber passes out from the heat and exertion. In other words, Moses does something that is not only at the limits of human endurance but also seems unnecessary.

Another unusual narrative sequence appears in verses 12 and 21–22. In verse 12, having alerted Moses that God is about to descend on the mountain (presumably from heaven), Yahweh commands him to warn the people not to come up the mountain or even to touch it. The reason

Climbing Mount Sinai is no easy task.

given is that Yahweh is a holy God and this mountain is holy because of Yahweh's presence. But in verses 21–22, Yahweh essentially issues the same command to a surprised Moses who then reminds Yahweh that the prohibition was given already. This may be the only place in the Bible where it is necessary to remind God of a divine decree (and this one only recently issued).

Still another incongruity lies in the disturbances of nature that accompany God's appearance on the mountain. Verse 16 portrays a thunderstorm (rare for the Sinai desert), whereas verse 18 appears to be describing an earth-shaking volcano.

There are other rough edges to the text, but these are sufficient to illustrate the difficult nature of this material from a narrative standpoint. As mentioned above, many are convinced that a variety of authors contributed to Exodus 19, but there is little agreement as to how the composition of the chapter relates to the larger literary history of the book of Exodus.

Was Mount Sinai volcanic?

The exact location of Mount Sinai is unknown, so the question cannot be answered. However, within the mountains near the southern portion of the Gulf of Aqabah are some believed to have been volcanic during biblical times. This description of the meteorological disturbance on the mountain is perhaps metaphorical, using stock phrases for appearances of God. Compare Judges 5:4–5 and Psalm 29.

From the Sea to Sinai

After the Israelites safely cross the Red Sea, the people wander in the wasteland to the east of the sea, and they complain to Moses about the quality of their drinking water (15:22–27) and about their lack of food (16:1–3). Yahweh responds to both crises, in the latter instance by sending manna (meaning in Hebrew "What is it?"—16:15) and quails for the people to eat (16:13).

On they move into the wilderness of Sin (or Zin), where the people argue with Moses again about water (17:1–7)—so much so, in fact, that Moses appeals to Yahweh for help: "What shall I do with this people? They are almost ready to stone me" (17:4). Yahweh directs Moses to strike the rock with the same staff he stretched over the Red Sea waters. When Moses does, this water obeys his will as well—gushing forth for the parched throats of the people. The place is named Massah

---

"Give us this day our daily bread."
—Matthew 6:11, NRSV

(meaning "to test," because this was a test of Yahweh by a sinful people) and Meribah (meaning "to quarrel"). The book of Numbers (20:1–13) records a similar incident, also in the wilderness of Zin at a place named Meribah, where Moses strikes the rock to obtain water for a thirsty Israel. This latter incident seems to be involved in the statement by Yahweh in Deuteronomy 32:51–52. There Yahweh considered Moses' striking of the rock as irreverent, and so the great leader of Israel is not allowed to enter the Land of Promise, but must die east of the Jordan River-Dead Sea valley. And so, according to Deuteronomy 32, it is the sour mood of the people that contributes to Moses' death, but in a quite different manner than Moses fears in Exodus 17:4.

Verses 8–16 of Exodus 17 contain a brief account of hostilities with the Amalekites. These verses are noteworthy not only because they recall a long and unhappy experience Israel has with these seminomadic people (see 1 Samuel 30), but also because they contain the first reference to Joshua, the strong leader who will assume Moses' office upon the latter's death (Deut. 34:9).

> "Forty years of tramping around the wilderness with the Israelites was enough to take it out of anybody. When they weren't raising hell about running out of food, they were raising it about running out of water. They were always hankering after the fleshpots of Egypt and making remarks about how they should have stayed home and let well enough alone." —Frederick Buechner, *Peculiar Treasures: A Biblical Who's Who* (San Francisco: Harper & Row, 1979), 111.

The visit of Jethro to Moses (Ex. 18:1–27) recalls how Moses first stumbled upon the holy power of Mount Horeb/Sinai (Ex. 3:1). That holiness is soon to be a primary focus of the text again, and the appearance of Jethro sets the stage for the reintroduction of that element in the story. But Jethro's return in Exodus 18 also foreshadows Moses' new responsibilities, as one who passes on to Israel God's covenant law. Here, the father-in-law gives valuable advice to Moses about delegating the enormous tasks involved in administering justice to the people.

The Israelites Reach Mount Sinai

The tangled narrative flow of Exodus 19 may have caused various interpreters to identify different divisions within the chapter. Although the NRSV introduces a paragraph break at verse 7, the initial subsection of Exodus 19 could be verses 1–8. Several reasons suggest that this subsection may act as an introduction to the rest of the book of Exodus. For instance, the first two verses provide two orientations: temporal and geographical. This pair of sentences (19:1–2) first provides a temporal orientation for what is about to take place. Three months to the day after the miracle at the Red Sea, the people arrive at Mount Horeb/Sinai. Many scholars see verse 1 as an indication of an annual festival to commemorate the appearance of God to Moses on this mountain. Though no specific description appears elsewhere in the Old Testament, this festival might well have been observed at one time or another in Israel's later life.

In addition, Exodus 19:1–2 provides a geographical orientation for the balance of Exodus. As noted, the Israelites have left the wilderness of Sin (or Zin) and arrived at the wilderness of Sinai, where they camp at the foot of the mountain. All that transpires from 19:2 through chapter 40, and on into the books of Leviticus and Numbers (specifically to Num. 10:11), will take place here, in the vicinity of this holy mountain.

A second reason for considering verses 1–8 as a prelude to all that follows is that these verses anticipate and summarize what lies ahead in the experience of the people. One brief example: In verse 8, the people promise Moses that "Everything that the LORD has spoken we will do." However, apart from Yahweh's demand that they "obey my voice and keep my covenant" (v. 5), Yahweh has not yet told the people what is expected of them. The Ten Commandments (20:1–17) have yet to be delivered, and the same may be said of the other legal material that follows in Exodus 21 and beyond. Clearly the people's response in verse 8 is in *anticipation* of what Yahweh is about to command them, and in an important respect, is also a *preparation* of the reader for an encounter with Yahweh's commands.

> "It belongs to the essence of faith that [one] accepts God's will *before* its implications have been made clear." —H. L. Ellison, *Exodus,* Daily Study Bible (Philadelphia: Westminster Press, 1982), 101.

Verse 3 identifies this subsection as a conversation between Yahweh and Moses, a conversation that has been initiated by Yahweh and whose purpose is to convey Yahweh's understanding of the significance of the impending events in the lives of these newly liberated slaves. Yahweh first reminds Moses and the people of the profound nature of God's providential care (v. 4). The reference to "eagles' wings" here is at the same time an image of tenderness and strength, and it recalls the haunting question of Exodus 15:11:

64

> Who is like you, O Yahweh, among the gods?
> Who is like you, majestic in holiness,
> awesome in splendor, doing wonders?

And perhaps this reference to eagles' wings in Exodus 19:4 was in the mind of Second Isaiah as he addressed another group of exiles, those who were deported to Babylon in the sixth century B.C.

> . . . those who wait for Yahweh shall renew their strength,
> they shall mount up with wings like eagles,
> they shall run and not be weary,
> they shall walk and not faint. (Isa. 40:31)

The strength of the Lord is itself a source of strength to those who appropriate it.

Yet the full force of verse 4 lies not only in the image of Yahweh as compassionate strength but also in the reason for this demonstration of divine protection: "I . . . brought you to myself." Israel has been saved for a purpose: to be the special people of Yahweh—a core theme of Exodus, which the text expands upon almost immediately.

The Conditions of the Covenant

Verse 5 is couched as a conditional statement, an instance of "if . . . then . . .": "If you obey my voice and keep my covenant . . ." The two phrases, "obey my voice" and "keep my covenant" are in reality two ways of saying the same thing. The text is in the process (Exodus 19–20) of explaining that Israel has a special relation with Yahweh unlike that of any other nation. For its part, Israel must live a certain way to maintain this relationship. The operative word is "covenant"—an agreement by two parties to live up to a mutually agreed upon set of principles. Although Israel does not yet know the principles, the framework of the agreement, the very nature of the covenant, is being spelled out here by Yahweh.

A few years ago, some scholars were struck by a remarkable similarity between the literary structure of certain parts of the Old Testament (including some of the material in Exodus 19–20) and the legal formula by which some of Israel's neighbors in the ancient world made treaties between themselves. These treaties often were drafted at the conclusion of a war in an effort to keep the peace or to impose the victor's will upon the defeated. In this setting, these agreements usually were not between equals, but between a sovereign party and a subservient party. These scholars pointed out that, in addition to certain other characteristics, the covenant depicted in Exodus 19–20 was like these ancient treaties. Of course, Yahweh had not defeated Israel, but the relationship was similar because Israel was a weak and dependent participant to the covenant while Yahweh was sovereign. The validity of this theory has been much debated among scholars, but the comparison does point to a very basic characteristic of Exodus 19–20: that Yahweh strikes a treaty, an agreement between God and Israel, in which both parties are active participants and the validity depends on the faithfulness of both parties to its conditions. (More about the "treaty formula" is in the following two sections.) This covenant is not new, but a renewal of an existing relationship that goes back to the time of Abraham (Genesis 15 and 17), indeed back to creation itself (Genesis 1). Exodus 3:15 and 6:2–4 are quite clear about that.

Yahweh Tells Moses the Conditions of the Covenant

A conceptual link exists between verses 5 and 6, though the NRSV translation divides them into separate verses. A schematic diagram of verses 5–6 (paraphrased) might look like this:

> If you obey my voice and keep my covenant, then:
>   you shall be my treasured possession out of all the peoples—
>   the whole earth is mine!—
>   you shall be for me a priestly kingdom,
>   you shall be a holy nation.

Each of these four "then" propositions deserves comment because here we stand at the heart of the Old Testament gospel, the good news that Israel has been chosen out of God's mercy to be the vehicle through whom all humankind will be blessed, enriched, and redeemed.

First

"You shall be my treasured possession out of all the peoples." National and ethnic groups in the ancient world commonly believed they had been singled out by their gods to receive special benevolence. The Egyptians particularly, whose geographical insularity seemed to be divinely endowed, had a strong sense of being chosen by the gods. Most Egyptians apparently took that fact for granted. Ancient Israel had to wrestle with what appeared to them to be a curious enigma. Ogden Nash's quip, "How odd of God to choose the Jews," was anticipated by ancient Israelites who could find no rhyme nor reason for their singularity before Yahweh. As they wrestled with the problem, an answer emerged which was as close to this mysterious truth as would ever be possible to get: God chose the Israelites simply out of mercy toward them. This is the way Deuteronomy 7:6–8 explains the first declaration of Exodus 19:5–6:

> Yahweh your God has chosen you out of all the peoples on earth to be his people, his treasured possession. It was not because you were more numerous than any other people that Yahweh set his heart on you and chose you—for you were the fewest of all peoples. It was because Yahweh loved you and kept the oath that he swore to your ancestors . . .

When probed to its deepest foundations, God's elective love for Israel is a wondrous mystery.

> "What does it mean to be God's redeemed people in the world? It is an invitation to be a people that carries forth God's purposes in the world." —Terence E. Fretheim, *Exodus*, Interpretation, 213.

Second

"The whole earth is mine." This statement seems an intrusion because it interrupts the symmetry of the other three propositions with their "you shall be" statements. Some scholars have identified this second proposition as a contribution by a zealous scribe who, while copying the text at a later time, wished to strengthen or "improve" it. Even so, the affirmation that "the whole earth is mine" is in complete harmony with the whole outlook of the book of Exodus. (See Fretheim, 212.) As noted earlier, this text echoes Israel's creation poetry, especially Genesis 1, which emphasizes the declaration that the God of the Red Sea miracle (and the God who is about to speak on Mount Horeb/Sinai) is the same God who presided over the creation of the heavens and the earth. In a world of competing gods, Exodus 19:5 goes out of its way to remind Moses (and us) that because Israel's God is also the creator, Israel's God is in possession of the heavens and the earth. Events—including the election of Israel—move along according to God's will. "He's got the whole world in his hands" is the song of Exodus 19:5.

Third

"You shall be for me a priestly kingdom." If the first proposition raises the question, "Why did God choose Israel?" the third proposition addresses the issue of why God would choose any nation. The key term here is the word "priestly," which connects to Israel's role as mediator of God's saving love to the larger world. Like many themes in Exodus, this one is not introduced into the text as a novelty, but as an older theme that is here given a fresh application. In the narrative from Genesis which recounts God's call to Abraham to leave his home to go to an undisclosed destination (Gen. 12:1–3), the purpose for Israel's greatest ancestor is clearly spelled out: "in you all the families of the earth shall be blessed." (Note Heb. 11:8–12.) In that same understanding, Israel here is described as a priestly nation. Through Israel, more than through any other national or ethnic group, God's love for all will be revealed and mediated.

Fourth

"You shall be a holy nation." Appropriately, a statement concerning Israel's holiness is the climax of verses 5–6. Holiness—God's as well as Israel's—pervades Exodus 19–20, as it pervades the entire book of Exodus. Holiness is a complicated concept, and functions on many levels throughout the Old Testament. What is said here should be considered a mere "scratching of the surface" of this key element in scripture. Holiness means at least two important things in Exodus 19–20.

> "It has been proposed that the common distinction between 'the holy, and the common or not-holy' be restated as a distinction between 'the holy, and the not-yet holy.'" —J. Gerald Janzen, *Exodus*, Westminster Bible Companion, 134.

First of all, to be holy means to be completely "other" than, or set apart from, created things. God is holy in that, as creator, God stands over and above what God has fashioned, and is independent of creation. Put differently, while the created world is dependent upon God for continued existence, God is not dependent upon the world. In this sense, to call God holy is to say that God is unique,

68

self-sustaining, and differentiated from anything in the created order—as in the refrain from Exodus 15:11: "Who is like you, O Yahweh . . .?"

To be holy also means to be moral. God is holy because God is morally consistent, embracing the same values today and throughout all the world's tomorrows. This does not mean that God is inflexible or unresponsive to human events, such as prayer (note Ex. 32:11–14, Amos 7:1–3, and elsewhere), but that as Israel's God embraces the realities of justice and compassion today, so this same God will embrace those identical qualities in perpetuity. In the example of Abraham and Sarah, these ancestors of Israel responded to God's call, not because their destination was in sight, but because they had learned that God could be trusted.

A fascinating thing about the "holy nation" proposition in Exodus 19:6 is that Israel is called to emulate God's holiness. Israel is to be holy—its special relationship to God makes Israel set apart from other nations. Israel is to be *in* this world, but not *of* this world. Equally important is the moral component of Israel's holiness. Israel is to be morally consistent, embracing the foundational values of justice and compassion, just as those values are embraced by Israel's holy God. To be sure, there is an important distinction between God's holiness and that of Israel. While God's holiness is an inseparable part of God's being, Israel's holiness is derived from the God who elects it. God cannot slough off from holiness, but Israel often does so through its sinful and disobedient ways. Yet God's challenge remains: "You shall be holy, for I Yahweh your God am holy" (Lev. 19:2; also see 20:7, and elsewhere). Later, Israel's prophets continue challenging Israel to live up to God's moral ideals because a holy God demands holy lives (see Isa. 6:1–13).

With the death and resurrection of Jesus Christ, the writers of the New Testament were convinced that the reality of Israel as a chosen and holy people had been bestowed upon the church. First Peter 2:9–10 borrows heavily upon the language of Exodus 19:5–6 to express this idea (the following translation is from the NRSV, according to that translation's marginal notation).

> But you are a chosen race, a royal priesthood, a holy nation, a people for his possession, in order that you may proclaim the mighty acts of him who called you out of darkness into his marvelous light.
>
> Once you were not a people,
> but now you are God's people;

69

once you had not received mercy,
but now you have received mercy.

The Narrative Conclusion

Verses 7–8 finish this subsection of Exodus 19. Following Yahweh's command, Moses descends from the mountain to communicate God's message to the people. They respond enthusiastically, even though they do not know God's demands of them. As noted, theologically, this casts all of Exodus 19 in the light of anticipation and preparation. Psychologically, the people's quick and uninformed response emphasizes their portrayal as being fickle and temperamental, ready to attempt the impossible one moment, yet fearful and complaining the next.

If there is a treaty formula in the literary structure of portions of Exodus, as some scholars assert, then 19:3–8 might be such a spot. As Childs points out (366), three distinct parts of this passage resemble the treaty or covenant formulation.

Verse 4: A statement of God's deeds in the past
Verses 5–6: The conditions ("If . . . then . . .") of the covenant
Verses 7–8: The agreement by the parties (implied, in the case of Yahweh)

Very likely, the legal material in Exodus 20:1–17 (the Ten Commandments), is a part of that by which Israel is bound to God by Yahweh, and by which Israel casts her destiny with her Lord.

Thunder on the Mountain

Though the theological and narrative agenda for what follows in Exodus has been set by 19:1–8, the balance of the chapter deserves a few comments. Verses 9–15 describe the manner in which (1) Yahweh reaffirms Moses' leadership so "that the people may hear when I speak with you and so trust you ever after" (v. 9), and (2) how the people—having been warned to stay off the mountain—prepare themselves for the awesome coming of their God. Moses "consecrates" them (literally: "makes them holy") and they acknowledge their participation in this momentous event by washing their clothes, an obvious symbol of their renewal.

The final subsection of Exodus 19 consists of verses 16–25, concerning events that occur on the "third day" (v. 16, note v. 15), or two days after the people arrive in the vicinity of the mountain (see 19:1). The theophany (an appearance by God) occurs in a crescendo of sight and sound—a thunderstorm and a volcanic eruption—which is accompanied by the shrill cry of the ram's horn, the sho-

> ". . . an atmosphere electric with Yahweh's presence." —John I. Durham, *Exodus*, Word Biblical Commentary, 271.

far (the "trumpet" of v. 19). Yahweh descends to the top of the mountain and is met by Moses. After the problematic conversation of verse 21–23, Yahweh commands Moses to return to the base of the mountain to get Aaron, who is to be present for the climactic moment. (Curiously, it is unclear if Aaron goes back up the mountain with Moses, as he is not mentioned again until Ex. 24:1.)

The situation is set, and everything is now in place, for what is perhaps God's most dramatic self-revelation in all the Old Testament: the giving of the law (Ex. 20:1–17).

Continuity with the New Testament

The narrative of Yahweh's appearance on Mount Horeb/Sinai is also in the background of another important New Testament passage, Hebrews 12:18–24. In speaking of those who have had an experience of Christ, the anonymous author of this letter reminds readers that they "have not come to something [some ancient New Testament manuscripts say: have not come to a mountain] that can be touched, a blazing fire, and darkness, and gloom, and a tempest, and the sound of a trumpet, and a voice . . ." (Heb. 12:18–19). To the

Want to Know More?

About manna? See Paul J. Achtemeier, ed., *Harper's Bible Dictionary* (San Francisco: Harper & Row, 1985), 600–601.

About holiness? See Achtemeier, *Harper's Bible Dictionary*, 400–401; Shirley C. Guthrie, *Christian Doctrine*, rev. ed. (Louisville, Ky.: Westminster John Knox Press, 1994), 337–48.

About the sin and punishment of Moses? See Thomas W. Mann, *Deuteronomy*, Westminster Bible Companion (Louisville, Ky.: Westminster John Knox Press, 1995), 33–34; Dennis T. Olson, *Numbers*, Interpretation (Louisville, Ky.: John Knox Press, 1996), 124–30.

About treaties in ancient times? See Dennis J. McCarthy, *Old Testament Covenant: Survey of Current Opinions* (Richmond: John Knox Press, 1972), 10–34; see also Dennis J. McCarthy, *Treaty and Covenant* (Rome: Pontifical Biblical Institute, 1972).

contrary, they "have come to Mount Zion and to the city of the living God, the heavenly Jerusalem, and to innumerable angels in festal gathering . . . and to Jesus, the mediator of a new covenant"

(12:22–24). In this interesting passage, one finds both continuity and discontinuity in the comparison between the new Israel (the church) and the old. The God of Mount Horeb/Sinai is the same as the God and Father of Jesus Christ, but the revelation in Christ is more complete than that to Moses. The same God now "speaks a better word" (v. 24) than before.

The writer of Hebrews 12 goes on to remember the earthquake that accompanied the volcano in Exodus 19:18, and ties that memory to a statement from ancient Israel's prophetic literature about the shaking "of the heavens and the earth" (Hag. 2:6). This is compared to "a kingdom that cannot be shaken," a reference (like that of "innumerable angels in festal gathering" above) to the establishment of the kingdom of God at the end of human history. Thus the author of Hebrews 12 uses Exodus 19 as a point of reference to compare, both positively and negatively, the life of Israel-of-old with the Christian life of the present, and of that to come.

? Questions for Reflection

1. This passage is filled with beautiful images (bearing on eagles' wings, being a treasured possession of God, washing one's clothes in consecration, etc.) and strong conditions. Who are the participants in the covenant? What are the conditions? What are the benefits? How do these conditions and benefits apply today?
2. Again, the themes of creation and promise, as well as continuity and discontinuity, are present in this passage. What are some of the examples of these themes?
3. Verse 8 is a record of the people's oath to follow God's words. Exodus has shown already that the Israelites are "prone to wander," and it will show shortly that their pattern of behavior will continue. How would you evaluate their ability to keep their commitments? What can help make commitments last?
4. In this passage, God's appearance is described in terms of thunder and lightning. In our day and age, thunder and lightning are often associated with elements of destruction. What language would you use to describe God?

7

The Ten Commandments: Part One

The Ten Commandments are one of the modern world's prevailing influences. This is not because people in our time are more dedicated to living by the Ten Commandments but because the image of the Ten Commandments inhabits our consciousness as a strong symbol of what is enduring and just. The persistent nature of this image means that statues of Moses and representations of the twin tablets of stone on which the commandments were written (Ex. 24:12) can be found in many public places—not only in synagogues and churches, where we might expect them, but in schools, libraries, courtrooms,

The image of the Ten Commandments is unmistakable, even to a child.

and other public buildings (sometimes causing controversy). Even Hollywood has understood the cinematic power of Moses and the Ten Commandments.

This attention is not difficult to understand. The Ten Commandments represent a conviction that in a world of changing values and constantly reinterpreted codes of human law, a moral dimension of life transcends the shifting sands. Human life should be lived within a framework of eternal moral values that transcend the moment and endure for all time and circumstance. These values are "written in stone," and therefore are inflexible, imperishable, and permanent. Indeed, the more "relative" contemporary human moral and ethical judgments become—or at least, the more they are perceived to be so—the more energetically some turn to the Ten Commandments as an "absolute" standard by which to judge human thought and conduct.

Many will agree that we live in a moral universe whose roots are found in the mind of God. However, the permanence and finality of the Ten Commandments may not be absolute. Even within the Bible, they have been subjected to various interpretations. Not surprisingly then, the Ten Commandments are viewed quite differently by various postbiblical interpreters—Jewish and Christian alike. To understand how the commandments have been "read" over the centuries, as well as how the commandments relate to a transcendent moral law that comes from God, the background behind the Ten Commandments must first be examined. Then we can look at each commandment to discover what it may have meant to ancient Israel as well as its meaning for our generation.

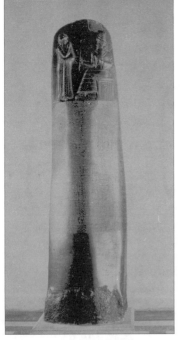

The stele of Hammurabi inscribed with Hammurabi's Code

The Context of the Ten Commandments

The larger world of ancient Israel was one pervaded by a sense of law. This was true in Mesopotamia (modern Iraq), that region out of which Abraham and Sarah traveled to the Land of Promise and to which ancient Israel always felt a sense of kinship (note, for example, Deut. 26:5). Thousands of years before Moses, formal codes of law appeared in Mesopotamia, the most famous of which is associated with the eighteenth century B.C. ruler of Babylon, Hammurabi. Hammurabi's Code, which may be seen on a beautifully engraved column of stone in the Louvre museum in Paris, bears striking resemblances to the Ten Commandments in several respects. In addition to containing some of the same legal provisions—against murder, for example—Hammurabi's Code is considered to be a gift from the gods, in this instance from the Mesopotamian god of justice, Shamash.

There are important differences between Hammurabi's Code and the Ten Commandments. First, while Hammurabi's Code may consider itself god-given, its emphasis is upon keeping order in Hammurabi's kingdom. An extended prologue devotes considerable energy to describing the greatness of the king and the importance of his political achievements. By comparison, the succinct prologue to the Ten Commandments focuses attention exclusively upon the saving grace of the God of Israel: "I am Yahweh your God, who brought you out of the land of Egypt, out of the house of slavery" (Ex. 20:2). This is one of the indications that the Ten Commandments are a covenant document, part of the agreement by which Yahweh and Israel are linked.

Another important difference is the manner in which their legal pronouncements are formulated. Like many other codes of law from the ancient world, including some to be found in the Bible (for example, Exodus 21–23), Hammurabi's Code is couched in a series of conditional statements. "If such and such a crime is committed, then thus and thus will be the punishment." The Ten Commandments, on the other hand, are consistently declaratory. "Remember the sabbath day . . . You shall not murder . . ." and so on. Undoubtedly this *un*conditional nature of the Ten Commandments has shaped their reputation as being inflexible and timeless, as well as the statement in Exodus 20:1 that the commandments represent the very words of the God of Israel.

Importance in the Hebrew Bible

In the Old Testament, the Ten Commandments are referred to as the "Ten Words" (Deut. 4:13 and elsewhere), a phrase whose English equivalent (by way of the Greek language) is "Decalogue," a term often applied to the Ten Commandments in our time. Also in the Old Testament (although not in Exodus 20), the commandments are portrayed as having been written by the finger of God on two stone tablets. Furthermore, many ancient Israelites considered the commandments as God's ultimate will for human life and conduct. They are repeated, for example, in Deuteronomy 5:6–21 in substantially the same words. In addition, certain texts from the prophets point to the importance of the Ten Commandments in the view of these courageous spokespersons for Israel's God. The eighth-century B.C. prophet Hosea, who had a particularly deep admiration for Moses and the exodus generation (note Hos. 11:1; 12:13; and elsewhere), uses the commandments to describe the sinful ways of his own generation:

> Swearing, lying, and murder,
>   and stealing and adultery break out;
>   bloodshed follows bloodshed. (Hos. 4:2; compare Jer. 7:9)

A final example of the Commandments' significance to other parts of the Old Testament can be found in Psalm 81. This psalm celebrates the exodus experience, including a quotation (Ps. 81:10) of the prologue to the Ten Commandments found in Exodus 20:2.

The Commandments Themselves

In spite of the persistent memory of the significance of the Ten Commandments, Israel did not always understand the individual commandments in the same way from generation to generation, as noted at the beginning of this discussion.

There is not universal agreement on how the commandments should be numbered. In the discussion below, Exodus 20:3 is regarded as the First Commandment, although some faith traditions consider this verse to be part of a single commandment contained in verses 3–6 (considered here as the First and Second Commandments). Those who follow this latter enumeration usually consider Exodus 20:17 to comprise the Ninth *and* Tenth Commandments, so that the total number comes to the required ten. In our discussion, Exodus 20:17 in its entirety is considered the Tenth Commandment. All of this is simply arithmetic, and has no bearing on the contents of the Commandments or their value for modern life.

> "If working for six days and resting on the seventh images the God who in six days created heaven and earth and rested on the seventh, can we say more generally that as we respond to God through lives shaped by the Ten Commandments, we image God?" —J. Gerald Janzen, *Exodus, Westminster Bible Companion*, 141.

The First Commandment

"You shall have no other gods before me" (Ex. 20:3). Ancient Israel lived in a world teeming with deities, or at least it seemed that way because of the multiplicity of gods worshiped by the Egyptians, Babylonians, Canaanites, and Israel's other neighbors. Many ancient people believed that each nation owed special allegiance to a particular deity who served as the patron and protector of that nation: for example, Amon for the Egyptians, Baal for the Canaanites, and so on. Because of this special linkage, gods often were considered to be territorial—that is, they were believed to preside over a specific nation's real estate because of their special alliance with the people who lived there. When the Syrian general Naaman traveled to Israel to be cured of leprosy by the prophet Elisha, he declared his undying faithfulness to Israel's God and his intention to worship this God by taking home with him a bit of Israelite soil. "Please let two mule-loads of earth be given to your servant; for your servant will no longer offer burnt offering or sacrifice to any god except Yahweh" (2 Kings 5:17). In other words, Yahweh could only be worshiped in Yahweh's land, even if this "land" consisted of only a small pile of Israelite clay deposited in far-off Syria.

The God of Israel portrayed in Exodus is a very different kind of God. This is a God who is not confined to national borders or to any particular cultural or political configuration. This God turns the waters of the Nile to blood and confounds the best skills of the magician-priests of Egypt's gods. This is the God who separates the waters of the Red Sea and drowns the army of Pharaoh. This is a God who is totally unlike any other god and is sovereign over them all, who owns no land (except in the sense of a land promised to the Israelites) because the whole earth is Yahweh's. The First Commandment is an imperative laid upon Israel not to forget this reality in how the nation thinks about God or how the nation lives its life. Yahweh is supreme. On that reality the nation's life is based, and on that reality all the other commandments are based.

Exodus 20:3 is a statement about how God's people should order their priorities. Yahweh must be first and last; Yahweh foremost of all. But is this also a statement that no other god exists? In other words, is the First Commandment a call to monotheism?

That is not an easy question to answer, and it is one that scholars have debated for some time. On the one hand, clearly a monotheistic commitment to Yahweh plays a crucial role in the thought of the prophets. One need only read Isaiah 44:9–20 and its comic mockery of those who make and worship idols to realize that. (By the way, who ever said that nothing in the Bible is funny?) On the other hand, no statement is made in Exodus which explicitly denies the existence of Egypt's gods. In fact, as noted earlier, the contest between Moses and Pharaoh is, in a very real sense, a contest between Yahweh and the gods of Egypt. This portrayal would seem to imply that, although they would prove to be subservient to Yahweh, the gods of Egypt were authentic realities. Perhaps Moses and his contemporaries could be categorized as "henotheists." That is, they would not deny that other gods exist, but they affirmed the authority of Yahweh alone in their lives and to Yahweh they gave their total commitment.

Key Terms

transcendent Over and beyond all things, usually in reference to God, who is superior in all ways to all things.

monotheism Belief in one god.

henotheism The belief that while many gods may exist, there is one god who is supreme over them. Henotheism is sometimes used synonymously with *monolatry* (the selection of one god even though many gods may exist).

icon A religious image on a panel, used in the devotional practices of Eastern Christian (Orthodox) traditions. Icons are understood as windows from this reality into the eternal, and thus, one "sees through" an icon.

The monotheist-henotheist debate can be left to the historians of religion because, regardless of how the debate turns out, the meaning of the First Commandment is unequivocal: "Worship the Lord your God, and serve only him," as Jesus was later to say to Satan (Matt. 4:10; see Deut. 6:13). In other words, it is a statement about where Israel's ultimate priority should lie, the nation's ultimate commitment. And, as Jesus' words remind us, it is also a statement about the commitment of anyone who would be a disciple of Christ.

The Second Commandment

"You shall not make for yourself a graven image, or any likeness. . . (20:4–6, RSV). The RSV translation is cited here, instead of NRSV, for two reasons. First, the Hebrew word *pesel*, translated "image" (RSV) or "idol" (NRSV), seems really to mean "something that is carved or shaped" (thus RSV's use of the obsolete term "graven image," the equivalent in modern terms of "chiseled portrait"). In other words,

"Maybe God addresses the problem of idolatry at the outset of a new relationship with Israel because human beings are incurable and inventive idol-makers." — Kathleen Norris, *Amazing Grace: A Vocabulary of Faith* (New York: Riverhead Books, 1998), 91–92.

pesel has a more inclusive meaning than "idol" and also may mean something religiously neutral like "statue" or "carving." (For example, the verb form of the word is used in 1 Kings 5:18 to describe the work of Solomon's stonemasons.) Second, the NRSV translation of Exodus 20:4 is, in reality, a translation of Deuteronomy 5:8 (the Second Commandment in Deuteronomy's listing), which, in the Hebrew, seems to speak of the "likeness" ("of anything that is in heaven above," etc.)

as being another term for *pesel,* whereas the RSV accurately reflects the Hebrew of Exodus 20:4 in understanding "image" and "likeness" as two related, but distinct, objects of the verb "make." In other words, while Deuteronomy 5:8 commands "You shall not make for yourself a *pesel,* whether in the form of anything that is in the heaven above . . . ," Exodus 20:4 enjoins: "You shall not make for yourself a *pesel,* nor (shall you make) a likeness . . ." (author's translation). This is not just a splitting of verbal hairs, as we shall attempt to demonstrate in just a moment.

Regardless of the manner in which one translates the Hebrew of either Exodus 20:4–6 or Deuteronomy 5:8–10, the basic injunction of the Second Commandment is that Israel must not attempt to worship Yahweh by means of any artistic or representational devices shaped by human hands. In other words, no matter what other nations may do, Israel should have no idols! "You shall not make [them]. . . . You shall not bow down to them or worship them."

Why that should be is a mystery. Many interpreters of this commandment have suggested that any humanly crafted likeness of God is bound to be a failure, and thus an irreverence. The reality of a transcendent God cannot be contained by anything of human manufacture. This line of reasoning is similar to that of those who maintain that any description of God couched in words must necessarily fall short of the mark because of the finite and limited nature of human language. For that reason, they describe what God is *not* rather than what God is. In much the same way, any likeness of God composed by a human artist must be a distortion.

Another possible explanation for the Second Commandment is that worship through idols places the worshiper in serious jeopardy of confusing the idol with the reality it is supposed to represent. That seems to be the thrust of the mocking comments in Isaiah 44:9–20.

All of these lines of argumentation may be relevant, but they do not seem to be the focus of the Second Commandment. The reason that Israel should make no idols, according to the text of 20:5, is this: "because I am Yahweh your God, a zealous God . . ." (author's translation). Childs points out that the Second Commandment somehow protected Yahweh's identity, and he suggests that Deuteronomy 4:9–20 contains the most ample interpretation of the Second Commandment to be found in the Old Testament (406–7). Verse 12 emphasizes that at Mount Horeb/Sinai, Israel never saw Yahweh, but experienced him as a voice only: "You heard the sound of words, but saw no form; there was only a voice." Yahweh is not a God who can be apprehended by human sight, but a God who *speaks* and who *acts* in the context of human life. Anything that reduces God to what can be seen and touched is a violation of God's essential nature and is therefore a violation of Yahweh's covenant with Israel (notice Deut. 4:12).

"Unlike plastic images, which are static and immobile, deaf and dumb, unfeeling and unthinking, and fix God at a point in time, Israel's God is one who can speak and feel and act in both nature and history (and in this sense is free)." —Terence E. Fretheim, *Exodus*, Interpretation, 226.

The text of Exodus 20:4–6 goes on to describe Yahweh as a "jealous God" (NRSV) whose judgment and/or mercy extends over the generations. The translation of the Hebrew word *kana'* as "jealous" is a time-honored one, going back at least to the King James translation of 1611. "Zealous" might be a more appropriate English term, not only because *kana'* sometimes means "zealous" (see 1 Kings 19:10), but also because since the Middle Ages, jealousy has been regarded as one of the seven deadly sins. So in one sense, "zealous" is a more palatable description than "jealous." But in another sense, Yahweh is quite jealous. In fact Yahweh will tolerate no apportionment commitment—no sharing of Israel's affection with any other god!

That Yahweh will continue to punish grandchildren and great-grandchildren for the sins of their ancestors (Ex. 20:5) has proved troublesome to more than one modern reader. Important to remember is that the Second Commandment is part of a covenant document between the community of Israel and its God. The role of the individual, as modern women and men understand it, was not fully developed. God's spokespersons after Moses' time, prophets like Jeremiah (Jer. 31:29–30) and Ezekiel (Ezek. 18:2–4), begin to set forth an understanding of the significance of individual persons before God. So the implications of the anger and love of God described in 20:5–6 are best understood when tied to the results *within the community* of Israel's faithfulness (or lack thereof) over the years.

This consideration of the Second Commandment began with a somewhat technical discussion of the proper translation of the Hebrew term *pesel* and the structure of the sentence contained in 20:4. The reason for that discussion is that there is good evidence that ancient Israel understood the Second Commandment to prohibit not just religious idols but *any* artistic representations—in other words, a prohibition against "any likeness of anything that is in heaven above . . ." Archaeology has revealed precious few statues or portraits of humans or animals from the soil on which ancient Israel lived.

Some of those that have been discovered were probably representative of a heterodox religious ritual like the golden calves of Exodus 32:1–6 and 1 Kings 12:28. To be sure, there are a few references to the work of the engraver, such as the carved cherubim, palm trees, and flowers mentioned in 1 Kings 6:35. Not a single portrait of a biblical personality (including a New Testament personality) is known to exist which was executed during or near the lifetime of the individual, the single exception being a small relief carving of King Jehu (2 Kings 9–10) chiseled out by the artisans who worked for the Assyrian king Shalmanesser III (858–824 B.C.). (The religious art of Islam to this day is almost devoid of any pictorial representation of a human being—and certainly none of God—with the result that many mosques are ornamented with what must rank among the world's most beautiful examples of calligraphy—texts from the Koran written in gorgeously decorated script.)

In the Christian tradition there has been widespread disagreement—often actual conflict— over the matter of images of God, Jesus, and the saints. Some Protestant groups, especially within the Calvinistic tradition, regarded any image of God or Jesus as sinful. This view gave birth to the simple, unadorned beauty of the Puritan churches of New England. In contrast, others like those in the Orthodox and Roman Catholic traditions, placed great emphasis on the use of icons. They have

Want to Know More?

About the commandments discussed in this unit? See J. Gerald Janzen, *Exodus*, Westminster Bible Companion (Louisville, Ky.: Westminster John Knox Press, 1997), 140–48; Thomas W. Mann, *Deuteronomy*, Westminster Bible Companion, 49–73; Albert Curry Winn, *A Christian Primer: The Prayer, the Creed, the Commandments* (Louisville, Ky.: Westminster John Knox Press, 1990), 185–213.

About Hammurabi? See John Bright, *A History of Israel*, 3d ed. (Philadelphia: Westminster Press, 1981), 58–59; Paul J. Achtemeier, ed., *Harper's Bible Dictionary*, 370–71.

About the deities of other ancient peoples? See the listings for individual gods like Baal, Marduk, Serapis, and so on, in a good Bible dictionary like Achtemeier, *Harper's Bible Dictionary*; also see Keith Crim, ed., *The Interpreter's Dictionary of the Bible*, Supplementary Volume (Nashville: Abingdon Press, 1976), 222–25; or (if available) Robert M. Grant, *Gods and the One God*, Library of Early Christianity (Philadelphia: Westminster Press, 1986), 19–71.

About henotheism and monotheism? See Alan Richardson and John Bowden, eds., *The Westminster Dictionary of Christian Theology* (Philadelphia: Westminster Press, 1983), 248–49 and 381–82; Werner H. Schmidt, *The Faith of the Old Testament: A History* (Philadelphia: Westminster Press, 1983), 69–77.

About the prohibition of images? See Schmidt, *The Faith of the Old Testament*, 77–84.

About icons? See Jim Forest, *Praying with Icons* (Maryknoll, N.Y.: Orbis Books, 1997); Henri J. Nouwen, *Behold the Beauty of the Lord: Praying with Icons* (Notre Dame, Ind.: Ave Maria Press, created an artistic medium of undeniable power and majesty. The controversy over the matter has been more subdued in our own time, so that Christians who have different histories can draw appreciation and strength from one another. One would hope that few Christians of today would deny the quiet, uncomplicated dignity of a Quaker meeting house, or, when gazing at the magnificent portrait of God raising Adam to life on the ceiling of the Sistine Chapel, would accuse Michelangelo of violating the Second Commandment.

"God is spirit, and those who worship him must worship in spirit and truth" (John 4:24). That is the point of the Second Commandment.

The Third Commandment

"You shall not make wrongful use of the name of Yahweh your God . . ." (Ex. 20:7). Early in Exodus, two texts direct the attention of the reader to the significance of God's name. Moses' first encounter with God, as described in Exodus 3 (see unit 2), reaches a climax when Moses is commissioned by God to go to Pharaoh to demand the freedom of the Israelite slaves. A profoundly shaken and doubting Moses not only asks for evidence that his experience of this Presence in the burning bush is really what it seems to be, but also he wants to know God's name (3:13). On the surface, this request appears to be for purposes of simple identification. In reality, both he and the Israelites gain some of this God's power and authority. To know God's name was, in a very authentic sense, to know God. Also, in Exodus 6:1–3, God instructs Moses that, even though the earliest ancestors of Israel knew this God to be their own, Moses is being given a deeper insight into the nature of God. God's name, Yahweh, is now revealed for the first time. The strong implication of the text is that to know God as Yahweh is to enjoy a relationship with God which was not even accorded Abraham, Sarah, and their immediate descendants. The name of God has crucial significance for ancient Israel.

One popular way of looking at the Third Commandment is to consider this statement within a legal context. In other words, this commandment is seen as a warning against perjury. Every civilized society places importance on people speaking the truth. In order to ensure that they do, certain rituals are used which have deep religious implications. In Genesis 24, for example, when Abraham wishes to ensure that his servant will carry out his wishes with respect to obtaining a wife for Isaac, Abraham says:

> Put your hand under my thigh, and I will make you swear by Yah-weh, the God of heaven and earth, that you will not get a wife for my son from the daughters of the Canaanites, among whom I live, but will go to my country and to my kindred and get a wife for my son Isaac. (Gen. 24:2–4)

With slight adjustments (a hand on a Bible instead of under the thigh [that is, near the genitals, the seat of life]) this ceremony is al-most identical to the oath taken in a modern American courtroom or upon the occasion of the inauguration of a new President.

This manner of understanding the Third Commandment is to "read" it, "If one invokes God's name in taking an oath, one must be sure to tell the truth." Leviticus 19:12 appears to have this interpre-tation in mind: "You shall not swear falsely by my name, profaning the name of your God: I am Yahweh." Jesus, of course, will look for-ward to a day when oaths are unnecessary: "I say to you, Do not swear at all. . . . Let your word be 'Yes, Yes' or 'No, No'; anything more than this comes from the evil one" (Matt. 5:33–37). The Third Commandment realizes that humans have not reached that point yet, and thus issues a warning against perjury in the name of God.

While few doubt that a legal rationale is involved in Exodus 20:7, the Third Commandment probably contains a broader application, one suggested by the NRSV translation cited above. Yahweh is the sovereign Lord of all of life. Any reference to God's name that fails to do justice to that reality inflicts in-jury upon God and upon God's relation to the world. Centuries after Moses, the writers of the book of Deuteronomy understood the all-pervasive presence and authority of God's name. In some texts, God's "name" becomes a symbolic reference for God. For example, in de-scribing how Israel should assemble for worship, Deuteronomy 12:5 directs: "You shall seek the place that Yahweh your God will choose out of all your tribes as his habitation to *put his name* there." Understood in this light, the Third Commandment is an injunction against using God's

> "At the deepest level, use of God's name is a matter of mission. . . . God's name is to be used in prayer and praise, one impor-tant dimension of which is witness. Many psalms do so: . . . 'For this I will extol you, O LORD, among the nations, and sing praises to your name' (Psalms 18:49)." — Terence E. Fretheim, *Exodus*, Interpreta-tion, 228–29.

name wrongfully. To do so is an attempt to manipulate and subvert God.

[*Note:* The discussion of the Ten Commandments continues in unit 8.]

? Questions for Reflection

1. How have the Ten Commandments affected human history (either religious or secular)? What are your feelings about the importance of the Ten Commandments?
2. These first few commandments focus on prohibitions about other gods and idols. What are some of the "other gods" in our day and age? How are we tempted to follow or worship them? What makes these gods appealing to us?
3. On page 92 of her book *Amazing Grace: A Vocabulary of Faith* (New York: Riverhead Books, 1998), Kathleen Norris comments that even religion can become an idol. What do you think she means by that?
4. What are ways we can misuse the name of the Lord? Use this unit's discussion of the Third Commandment as a help.

The Ten Commandments: Part Two

The first three commandments deal with God's nature and the manner in which Israel must order its priorities and worship so as not to violate God's essential character. The final six commandments deal with interpersonal relations within the covenant community, or how people should treat one another. The Fourth Commandment functions as a bridge between these two sections. This commandment sets aside a special day in acknowledgment of God's activity in human life, and speaks a word to the community about the conduct of individual Israelites (". . . you, your son or your daughter . . ."). In other words, the commandment is about both worship (although worship is not specifically mentioned in the text) and daily life.

The Fourth Commandment

"Remember the sabbath day, and keep it holy . . ." (Ex. 20:8–11). The Fourth Commandment has several distinctions. First, along with the Fifth Commandment, this commandment is couched in positive terms. Second, this commandment is the longest of the commandments, containing fifty-

"And indeed, it was very good." And God rested.

five Hebrew words, as opposed to the forty-three words of the Second Commandment. (The Sixth, Seventh, and Eighth Commandments contain only two Hebrew words each!) Third, in comparison with the wording in Deuteronomy 5:6–21, the Fourth Commandment shows the most divergent wording (compare Deut. 5:15 with Ex. 20:11). Whereas Exodus links the Sabbath observance to God's activity at creation, Deuteronomy finds the rationale for Sabbath observance in Israel's experience of slavery in Egypt.

At the heart of the commandment is an understanding of Yahweh's holiness (see the discussion of holiness in unit 6). Yahweh is holy, which means totally and completely "other." Yahweh is distinct from creation and is not dependent upon it in any way. Reflecting this sense of Yahweh's holiness, Israel is to set aside one day in seven to be distinct from the other six; to be totally "other." In the two parts of the sentence in 20:8, the second part is as important as the first: "Remember the sabbath day, and *keep it holy.*"

> "People are not to live as if all time were their own, to do with as they please. The God of all time retains the right to determine how one day shall or shall not be used." —Terence E. Fretheim, *Exodus,* Interpretation, 229.

As the vocabulary in 20:11 makes explicit, the Fourth Commandment in the Exodus version echoes the words of Genesis 1:1–2:4. Genesis 2:2–3 gives an understanding of the Old Testament understanding of the word "sabbath." In most English translations (including NRSV) we read that God "rested [Hebrew: *shabat*] on the seventh day from all the work that he had done." Though it is an accurate translation, unfortunately "rested" implies that God was tired and had to regroup before going on to the events described in Genesis 2–3 (the way we use the weekend to put ourselves back together to face Monday morning). A better translation of *shabat* is "desisted" or "held back" "from all the work that he had done." The reason God stopped working was not from exhaustion, but because the work was complete. It was perfect. No other creative activity was needed—until the ugly reality of human sin intruded.

Israel's Sabbath is not intended to be only a day of rest. Sabbath is a holy festival, observed in honor of the holy God who set the stars in their courses and the sea in its bed. Admittedly, rest becomes an important reason for Sabbath observance, a motivation suggested by Exodus 20:11, where the text does use an authentic Hebrew word for "rest" to describe the inactivity of God: "Yahweh . . . rested (*nuach*) on the seventh day . . ." But at the core, the Fourth Commandment implores Israel to keep the seventh day as a holy day, a celebration that a holy God has bonded to Israel and Israel to that God.

Within the Jewish community, Sabbath observance has been a prominent feature of the lives of the faithful. Much rabbinic commentary over the centuries has been devoted to what is and what is not proper for a good Jew to do on the Sabbath. Christians have emphasized not the last day of the week, but the first as a festival to Christ's resurrection, sometimes referred to as a Christian Sabbath, or more appropriately the Lord's Day. Jesus' comment in Mark 2:27–28 has influenced this shift. When challenged by his enemies that his disciples were violating the Sabbath by gathering food, Jesus observes that "the sabbath was made for humankind, and not humankind for the sabbath; so the Son of Man is lord even of the sabbath." By these words, Jesus also signaled that freedom is an important element in the Christian attitude toward the law.

The Fifth Commandment

"Honor your father and your mother . . ." (Ex. 20:12). Unlike modern Western society, ancient Israelite society linked family solidarity and economic well-being tightly together. The family typically owned a plot of land and the buildings on it. The property usually was handed down from generation to generation in the name of the oldest male. An excellent snapshot of this arrangement may be found in 1 Kings 21, a story where a family's right to its property is violated (note especially v. 3). If for some reason the title to the property was jeopardized, a male kinsman had the responsibility to step forward to save (or "redeem") the land. (For a good example, see Jer. 32:1–15 and note how Jeremiah, the "redeemer" in this incident, purchases the land of his cousin Hanamel.)

These arrangements worked well as long as all members of the family were able-bodied and could contribute to the work of the family farm. When the senior members of a family grew old and unable to work, they might be isolated from the fortunes of the rest of the family. Parental abuse was probably no worse in ancient Israel than in other societies, ancient or modern. However, ancient Israelite law is different because of its specific provision against parental abuse. The Fifth Commandment seems to have been directed originally toward the adult children of senior Israelites, ordering them not to abuse their parents, economically or otherwise. Interestingly, mothers as well as fathers are included in this command, a remarkable inclusion since women usually were considered the property of the dominant male.

As part of a covenant document, then, the Fifth Commandment preserved the cohesion of individual family units and helped preserve the integrity of the nation Israel—God's special family. That is without doubt the significance of the concluding clause of 20:12: "that your days may be long in the land that Yahweh your God is giving you."

This is the first commandment with a promise attached to it. It suggests that caring for one's aging parents encourages a climate whereby individuals and society will live longer. See Patrick D. Miller, *Deuteronomy*, Interpretation (Louisville, Ky.: John Knox Press, 1990), 85.

The Fifth Commandment is as valid for our time as for that of ancient Israel, but one must acknowledge that we live within very different economic and social structures. The abuse of parents by children is still possible, but we are painfully aware in recent years of the high incidence of abuse of children by their parents. There is no question that mutual love and care by all members of a family is the way to implement the provisions of the Fifth Commandment.

Jesus often had harsh words for those who attempted to fulfill one of the commandments in a narrow, legalistic sense, while violating its spirit. His remarks about the Fifth Commandment are no exception (note Mark 7:9–13). As Fretheim notes (231), honor is not a specific activity, but is an "open-ended" commitment involving "respect, esteem, . . . affection, considerateness, and appreciation." Perhaps the best understanding of the Fifth Commandment is to remember that when one honors parents, spouse, and children, one also honors God.

The Sixth Commandment

"You shall not murder" (Ex. 20:13). Scholars of the Ten Commandments have debated over the years the verb, pronounced *ratsach*, employed in the Sixth Commandment. Does it mean "to kill" (RSV) or, more specifically, "to murder" (NRSV)? It is not an easy question to answer because the Old Testament contains examples of use of *ratsach* which support either interpretation. Childs is undoubtedly correct (421) that the word experienced a change in meaning over the centuries. At an early stage in ancient Israel's life, *ratsach* referred to the killing of one person in retaliation for the killing of someone else (after the fashion of the Hatfields and the McCoys—a persistent problem in any tribal society). Ultimately the term came to mean any killing that was motivated by animosity and a wish to harm.

When viewed in this manner, the NRSV translation is probably the more accurate.

The scholarly debate over the Sixth Commandment has been paralleled by a more practical one. What constitutes "murder" in a biblical sense? Is it murder to kill another person in defense of one's own country or one's own home, even when under attack? There are those who have conscientiously concluded that it is. Is it murder to have an abortion, even if the mother's own life or health is threatened? There are those who believe that it is. Is it murder to terminate the life of a person by withholding life support systems, even in the face of that person's intense suffering and the inevitability of his or her death? Again, there are those who have decided that it is.

> **Isn't killing the first crime recorded in the Bible?**
>
> Remember Cain? God puts a mark on Cain so that no one who meets him will kill him. Perhaps this commandment is God's protective mark on our neighbor's forehead. —J. Gerald Janzen, *Exodus*, Westminster Bible Companion, 150–51.

But there are many who believe that there *can* be a just war, that abortion *is* permissible to save the life or health of the mother, that mercy (the Fifth Commandment?) *demands* no unnecessary suffering at the end of life.

These and other debates about the Sixth Commandment will continue far into the future as technology provides more and more life-or-death options. What is beyond dispute is that life is sacred. Life is a creation of God and a gift of God. Indeed, life is among God's most precious gifts, and therefore deserves a special kind of reverence. Life also deserves a special set of safeguards to ensure its preservation.

Jesus' comment on the Sixth Commandment is interesting and puzzling. "You have heard that it was said to those of ancient times, 'You shall not murder.'

> "In the taking of human life . . ., one acts in God's stead." —Terence E. Fretheim, *Exodus*, Interpretation, 233.

But I say to you that if you are angry with a brother or sister, you will be liable to judgment" (Matt. 5:21–22). Doesn't everyone get angry? Didn't Jesus himself get angry with the money changers in the Temple, for example (Mark 11:15–17), or with the Pharisees and Sadducees (Matt. 23 and elsewhere)? If everyone who gets angry is a murderer, then that must include us all.

However, Jesus must mean something other than "righteous indignation." The Greek word behind "angry" in Matthew 5:22 can mean the everyday anger we all feel, sometimes justifiably and sometimes not. The term can also mean "irascibility," a chronic ill will that results in constant suspicion of, and combat with, one's neighbor. Jesus seems to be saying that anger is a type of murder because it destroys the quality of life, even when not stilling a beating heart.

The Seventh Commandment

"You shall not commit adultery" (Ex. 20:14). The cultural world of ancient Israel is deeply ingrained in this commandment. Like the Fifth Commandment, it is intended to protect the solidarity of the family. Sexual relations in ancient Israel were considered to be legal and beneficial to the individuals involved only within the context of marriage. The laws concerning sexual conduct made important distinctions not only between married and unmarried persons but also between men and women. "Fornication" in the Bible applies to sexual intercourse between an unmarried woman and a man who can be either married or unmarried. While a serious offense (note Ex. 22:16–17 and Deut. 22:28–29), fornication is not considered as great a crime as adultery, which is sexual intercourse with a married woman (note Deut. 22:22). The apparent reason for this difference is that a married woman was considered the property of her husband.

For a married man to have sexual intercourse with an unmarried woman was a violation of her person, and that man had to marry the woman or pay compensation to her family (or both). But if a man had sexual intercourse with another man's wife, both offenders were to be killed, as the innocent man's marriage—and thus the solidarity of his family—had been violated.

The structures of modern family life are a world away from those of ancient Israel. Polygamy, common in the world of the Old Testament, has been banished from civilized society. The role of women, while still far from ideal, has improved by light-years when compared to women's role in the time of Hagar, Hannah, or Ruth and Naomi, to name but a few Old Testament women. Therefore the value of the Seventh Commandment has been questioned by more than one modern reader of the Bible, if for no other reason than that the grounds for understanding what constitutes adultery have changed so significantly.

Jesus' comments on the Seventh Commandment are helpful. In his critique of the Old Testament law in the Sermon on the Mount, Jesus states:

You have heard that it was said, "You shall not commit adultery." But I say to you that everyone who looks at a woman with lust has already committed adultery with her in his heart. (Matt. 5:27–28)

On the one hand, that statement reminds us that sinfulness is a matter, not just of what we do, but of how we think and feel. Our sinfulness is a matter of who we are, a matter of the heart. But on the other hand, there is scarcely a person alive who has not experienced lust. The force of Jesus' comment is not to help us avoid adulterous thoughts—they are all but inevitable—but to remind us that, since we are all adulterers-of-the-heart, we are all in need of the grace of God.

The Seventh Commandment continues to have value in our time in reminding us of the crucial nature of our family ties, which form the foundation of society. It also reminds us that marriage is a sacred institution—a sacrament for some Christians—and that marriage cannot be violated or abused without severe negative consequences to those parties involved, including children. Further, the Seventh Commandment reminds us that our sexuality is a potent force in our lives, capable of producing great joy or great sorrow. Our sexuality is one of the most awesome gifts with which God has endowed us.

> "Not only the act but the thought breaches the marriage vow." —Patrick D. Miller, *Deuteronomy*, Interpretation (Louisville, Ky.: John Knox Press, 1990), 90.

The Eighth Commandment

"You shall not steal" (Ex. 20:15). Some evidence exists that this commandment was once an injunction against kidnapping, that is, stealing a person. If so, it would parallel Exodus 21:16: "Whoever kidnaps a person, whether that person has been sold or is still held in possession, shall be put to death" (compare Deut. 24:7). However, in its present reading, the text is clearly a prohibition against any kind of theft. To some degree, this commandment anticipates and overlaps the Tenth Commandment.

Personal property was a valued commodity in Israel-of-old as it is today, perhaps even more so then in light of the general scarcity of wealth in the ancient world. Leviticus 19:13 makes it clear that ancient Israel considered the theft of another individual's goods a form of personal oppression. In other words, any act of theft violated the property owner's dignity and worth, and therefore violated the holiness of

Yahweh. Theft continued as a problem in ancient Israel, as evidenced by Hosea's inclusion of theft among his catalog of the people's sin (Hos. 4:2).

The Ninth Commandment

"You shall not bear false witness against your neighbor" (Ex. 20:16). Ancient Israel possessed a sophisticated justice system whereby plaintiffs brought their grievances against their fellow citizens or other judicial matters before a local tribunal consisting of village elders who met regularly at the city gate (note Ruth 4:1–12). In cases where one party felt that justice had not been served, appeals could be made to a priest. Many psalms, for example, reflect the voice of one who felt injured by others and by the judicial system itself. The cause (and the psalmist!) is placed in the hands of the priests, as a means of being placed also in the hands of God (Psalms 5, 9, 27, and elsewhere). As a strong central government developed under Kings David and Solomon, the royal authority extended to the appeals process. Solomon even constructed a "Hall of Judgment" (presumably a sort of supreme court) in the palace beside the new Temple in Jerusalem (1 Kings 7:7; see also the portrayal of the justice system in 1 Kings 3:16–28).

The judicial system had almost no physical or scientific evidence available, and therefore depended on the testimony of those who witnessed the criminal or civil matter under scrutiny. The integrity of the justice system, and the integrity of the nation's ordering of affairs, relied on the truth of the witnesses.

Various texts in the Old Testament point to the necessity of truth telling in courts of law. For example, in capital cases, no one could be convicted on the basis of one witness (Deut. 19:15, Num. 35:30). If a witness were caught lying, the punishment for the accused was inflicted on the liar (Deut. 19:19). It is not surprising that the Ten Commandments contain an injunction against perjuring oneself to the detriment of another.

The Ninth Commandment was given a broader application early in Israel's life. Truth telling was important in simple, everyday affairs and reflected the presence of Yahweh in the life of the covenant people: "You shall not lie to one another," declares Leviticus 19:11. A little further on in the text is: "You shall not go around as a slanderer among your people, and you shall not profit by the blood of your neighbor: I am Yahweh" (Lev. 19:16).

Remember the discussion earlier (unit 7) about Jesus and truth telling in Matthew 5:33–37, the thrust of which was that God's people should be so committed to speaking the truth that formal oaths would not be necessary. One's "yes" should mean yes, and one's "no," no.

The Tenth Commandment

"You shall not covet your neighbor's house . . ." (Ex. 20:17). Though similar to the Eighth Commandment, the Tenth is distinct from the Eighth because it deals not just with an external activity—theft—but with the inner motivation that leads to theft. To be honest before God, one must not even *want* to lay hands on another's possessions. If there is no covetousness, there will be no theft.

Does the Tenth Commandment also mean that we should not lust after our neighbor's house in the sense of wanting to build one like it (assuming, that is, that the house next door is grander and more comfortable than our own)? This commandment is often voiced this way in our time. In the presence of much unbridled greed and opulent consumerism in our society, this view has a certain authenticity. The love of money is, as 1 Timothy 6:10 reminds us, a root of much evil. But is this latter interpretation what the commandment actually intends? One must always confront the tension that, without a certain level of covetousness or greed, economic progress is not possible. What is clear is that, as the Eighth Commandment forbids theft, the Tenth Commandment condemns both theft and the impulses behind it.

> "[Covetousness] is the unbridled longing to possess more, the uncontrollable desire to possess things forbidden and which should not be desired at all." —William Barclay, *New Testament Words* (Philadelphia: Westminster Press, 1974), 61.

> "This is, of course, the outstanding sin of our time, and lies at the root of our social dissatisfaction and economic troubles." — H. L. Ellison, *Exodus*, Daily Study Bible (Philadelphia: Westminster Press, 1982), 115.

The Tenth Commandment anticipates the teachings of Jesus. For Jesus, keeping God's law was not dependent upon what one does, but upon what one thinks and feels, upon the condition of the heart (note Matt. 5:22 and 28).

Summary

The Old Testament gives strong evidence that the Ten Commandments are at the heart of Israelite law (note the legal provisions in
Exodus 21–23, Leviticus 17–26, and elsewhere). In the Jewish community, the collection of laws received the name *Torah*, a word that
is usually translated "law," but can actually mean something like
"leading" or "instruction." The name chosen to refer to Israel's God-
given law provides an important clue to the nature of these statues,
as understood by those who attempted to live by them. In the Old
Testament the Torah defines Israel; it sets this chosen-by-God nation
apart from all the rest; it identifies an individual as a Jew; and it provides Israel—both the nation and the individuals within it—with its
greatest joy.

Several texts in the Old Testament express the central role of the
Torah in Israel's life, and the great joy many individual Israelites
found in it. Noteworthy are three great "Torah psalms": 1, 19, and
119. Psalm 1 celebrates the Torah as the source of life within Israel,
in comparing the vitality of living with the Torah to the death that
occurs in the absence of Torah. Psalm 19 elevates God's gift of the
Torah to the status of the acts of God at creation, and places Torah
alongside the heavens and the sun as a witness to God's love and
compassion that caused the worlds to be.

Of the three psalms, Psalm 119 is the most interesting, if for no
other reason than its being the longest psalm in the Old Testament
(176 verses). In its lyric praise of the Torah, Psalm 119 contains these
sentiments:

> Open my eyes, so that I may behold
> wondrous things out of your law. (119:18)
>
> I will keep your law continually,
> forever and ever.
> I shall walk at liberty,
> for I have sought your precepts. (119:44–45)
>
> Oh, how I love your law!
> It is my meditation all day long. (119:97)

These examples (and there are others) demonstrate the deep, continuing love that Israel nurtured for the Torah. The reason for this
love is clear. The Torah was considered God's precious gift to the nation, a gift that allowed God's people to respond to God's redemp-

tive love. The Israel of the Old Testament—or at least those faithful individuals within Israel—experienced the law not as a constraint upon life but as a definition of human emotions and behaviors that lead to freedom and joy. It is not accidental that Psalm 119:45 equates Torah and liberty.

The New Testament presents a more complicated portrait of the Ten Commandments and Torah. Jesus refers to the law on many occasions, as the several references in our discussion to Matthew 5 have suggested. There Jesus makes clear that the Torah has not been superseded. On the contrary, Jesus himself fulfills the law (Matt. 5:17). Moreover, those who keep the law will do so not just in outward deeds but also in their hearts (5:22, 28, 44).

Perhaps Jesus' most definitive statement on the law comes in response to the question of a lawyer: "Teacher, which commandment in the law is the greatest?" In reply, Jesus quotes Deuteronomy 6:5 and Leviticus 19:18:

> "You shall love the Lord your God with all your heart, and with all your soul, and with all your mind." This is the greatest and first commandment. And a second is like it: "You shall love your neighbor as yourself." On these two commandments hang all the law and the prophets. (Matt. 22:34–40)

For his part, Paul has both positive and negative things to say about the Old Testament law. The law is good because it taught humankind our true nature before God, namely that we are sinners. In that sense, the law served as

 Want to Know More?

About the commandments discussed in this unit? See J. Gerald Janzen, *Exodus*, Westminster Bible Companion (Louisville, Ky.: Westminster John Knox Press, 1997), 148–58; Thomas W. Mann, *Deuteronomy*, Westminster Bible Companion (Louisville, Ky.: Westminster John Knox Press, 1995), 73–90; Albert Curry Winn, *A Christian Primer: The Prayer, the Creed, the Commandments* (Louisville, Ky.: Westminster John Knox Press, 1990), 214–57.

About Sabbath observance? See Rainer Albertz, *A History of Israelite Religion in the Old Testament Period*, vol. 2, Old Testament Library (Louisville, Ky.: Westminster John Knox Press, 1994), 408–11; Paul J. Achtemeier, ed., *Harper's Bible Dictionary* (San Francisco: Harper & Row, 1985), 888–89.

About the Sermon on the Mount? See the two chapters in Alyce M. McKenzie, *Matthew*, Interpretation Bible Studies (Louisville, Ky.: Geneva Press, 1998); Rudolf Schnackenburg, *All Things are Possible to Believers: Reflections on the Lord's Prayer and the Sermon on the Mount* (Louisville, Ky.: Westminster John Knox Press, 1995).

About the the Jewish judicial system? See Albertz, *A History of Israelite Religion in the Old Testament Period*, vol. 1, 91–94; Achtemeier, *Harper's Bible Dictionary*, 548–51.

About the status of women in Old Testament times? See Carol A. Newsom and Sharon H. Ringe, eds., *Women's Bible Commentary*, Expanded Edition (Louisville, Ky.: Westminster John Knox Press, 1998), 251–59; for a more technical treatment, see Gail Corrington Streete, *The Strange Woman: Power and Sex in the Bible* (Louisville, Ky.: Westminster John Knox Press, 1997); for an excellent, very readable treatment, see Evelyn and Frank Stagg, *Woman in the World of Jesus* (Philadelphia: Westminster Press, 1978).

our "disciplinarian" until the coming of Christ (Gal. 3:24). The law is evil because it is a curse, condemning us to death when we fail to live up to its provisions (Gal. 3:13). If not for Christ, we would remain in a state of death before God: "the law of the Spirit of life in Christ Jesus has set you free from the law of sin and death" (Rom. 8:2).

In Romans 13, Paul quotes from the Ten Commandments and concludes with words that come very near to Jesus' statement in Matthew 22. The Ten Commandments, Paul maintains, are summed up in this word, "Love your neighbor as yourself." Love does no wrong to a neighbor; therefore, love is the fulfilling of the law (Rom. 13:9–10).

Noted near the beginning of this discussion was the common perception that the Ten Commandments are the embodiment of an unchanging moral law written by God into the fabric of the universe. We also noted that the Ten Commandments have been variously interpreted and understood over the years. In the light of this contradiction, what should the Christian consider the law by which to live? Clearly for both Old and New Testaments—although in different ways—the key to the observance of the law lies in the word "freedom," a word that evokes both joy and terror. Observance is joy in the sense that one is freed from authoritarian shackles, and terror because the law now resides in the heart of the individual Christian.

Perhaps the last, best word in the matter was written by the great Latin theologian Augustine (died A.D. 430): "Dilige et quod vis fac," "Love, and do what you will." Augustine could make such a shocking declaration because he knew that if the heart is right—filled with love for God and love for neighbors—what we please to do will be consistent, insofar as it is humanly possible, with God's intentions for human life, and thus fulfill the law of Christ.

? Questions for Reflection

1. The Sabbath is to be kept holy. In the original understanding, the Sabbath would be Saturday, but Christians carry over the commandment to apply to Sunday. What does "holy" mean? How can we keep the Sabbath (or Sunday) holy?

2. The first commandments focused on relationship to God. These last few commandments speak to relationships with other people. How do we make the connection between our relationship to

God and relationships to others?

3. Perhaps more so than the other commandments, stealing can be a fuzzy issue. With photocopiers, VCRs, and the Internet, who can say what constitutes private property anymore? Imitation can be the highest compliment. How do you negotiate the line between what is stealing and what is not?

4. Jesus updates the commandments to apply them to our thoughts and attitudes, as well as our actions. What are some of the difficulties you face when you apply the commandments to thoughts and actions?

9 Exodus 32:1–35

The Golden Calf

Moses has been on the mountain now for "forty days and forty nights" (24:18), a symbolic biblical phrase meaning "a long time" (compare Gen. 7:12; Matt. 4:2). During this period, Yahweh expanded upon the basic Ten Commandments by delivering a more detailed series of laws, some of which spell out specifics already addressed in the Ten Commandments (Ex. 21:12, 22:1, and elsewhere), and some of which break new ground (21:18, 22:6, and elsewhere). These codes of law fall rather naturally into two groups: 20:22–23:33, which deal primarily with everyday matters, and 25:1–31:18, which deal with largely liturgical issues.

Between these sections, 24:1–18 describes a ceremony in which, in the presence of an awesome Yahweh (24:9–11, 16–17), the people accept the covenant that has been extended to them by their God. This ceremony is noteworthy not only because it reaffirms the covenant theme enunciated earlier in Exodus (see unit 6) but also for the following features:

1. "All the people" (24:3) assent to their bonding to Yahweh, and thereby fulfill what was anticipated in Exodus 19:8 (see unit 6).
2. The ceremony includes a reading of "the book of the covenant" (24:7), perhaps a reference to the Ten Commandments or 20:22–23:33, known as the Covenant Code.
3. Yahweh provides Moses with stone tablets inscribed with the Ten Commandments, which Yahweh has engraved "for their [the people's] instruction" (24:12; notice how 31:18 takes the

reader back to 24:12, thereby setting the stage for all that follows in 32:1–35).

4. Moses appoints Aaron and Hur to act as his deputies in his absence, and he advises the people: "Whoever has a dispute may go to them" (24:14). Little does Moses realize the sinister nature of the dispute that will eventually erupt.

The Mob Gets Ugly

Forty days and forty nights have become "a long time" indeed for the Israelites waiting impatiently at the foot of the mountain. The fickle and quick-tempered nature of the people has been emphasized already in Exodus (for example, 14:11–12), so not surprisingly, they gather menacingly around Aaron and demand action. "Get up" (this writer's translation). "Make for us gods who shall go before us; as for this Moses, the man who brought us up out of the land of Egypt, we do not know what has become of him." The text indicates that the people are dissatisfied with Yahweh because Yahweh's representative is absent.

> "When times get hard and God seems nowhere to be found, the consolations of what we can see and touch, taste and smell are awfully appealing: the feel of gold, the taste of skin, the smell of soil, the sea. Golden calves often beat out the impalpable God." —H. Stephen Shoemaker, GodStories: New Narratives from Sacred Texts (Valley Forge, Pa.: Judson Press, 1998), 84.

Aaron is easily intimidated, or else he too has begun to doubt Moses' return. He immediately acquiesces to the people's demand. He collects all their gold jewelry and melts down the mass of metal to fashion a calf of gold. (The Hebrew text is unclear whether Aaron melts the gold down to cast the calf in a mold, or sculpts it with a chisel or a knife. This distinction is unimportant because the point of vv. 3–4 is clear: Aaron took the people's gold and made a calf.) Then Aaron proudly proclaims: "These are your gods, O Israel, who brought you up out of the land of Egypt!"

The Calf of Gold

At this point at least two questions surface in the minds of many thoughtful readers. To what does the plural pronoun "these" refer? The narrative has described only a single golden calf. And is this calf intended as a substitute for Yahweh ("make gods for us"), or for Moses ("we don't know what has become of him"), or for both?

Neither question is easy to answer. For the first, some suggest the plural pronoun "these" has been influenced by the Hebrew word for

"God." *'Elohim* can mean "God" (32:16) or "gods" (32:1), and the translator knows which meaning to choose only by the larger context of the passage. (For various translations of this term, note the difference between Ps. 8:5 in standard English translations—including NRSV—and the manner in which the verse is quoted in Heb. 2:7.) Although unlikely, the pronoun may be plural in verse 1 in order to agree with *'elohim* in the same sentence. Then the translation would be: "This is your god, O Israel."

In Egypt, a bull was a sign of fertility.

More likely is the explanation that Exodus 32:1 has been influenced by 1 Kings 12:28, where an almost identical phrase appears in the context of a story in which there are *two* golden calves. Scholars long ago noticed similarities between the story of Aaron's golden calf and the narrative of the golden calves of Jeroboam I. Many have argued that there is a literary dependence in these two stories. Whether or not Exodus 32 was written with an eye directly on 1 Kings 12:28 is difficult to prove, but the possibility of some kind of influence is strong.

With regard to the second question (What does the golden calf represent?), Aaron must know he has violated the Second Commandment (making an image). Perhaps he is trying to avoid violating the First Commandment by not wishing to place an alien god alongside Yahweh. That appears to be demonstrated by his announcement immediately after the presentation of the calf to the people: "Tomorrow shall be a festival to Yahweh" (v. 5). He seems to be directing the people away from the conclusion that the calf is a different god than Yahweh. And so what is it intended to be?

The issue is clouded by the wording of the original demand of the people in verse 1. They demand someone or something "who shall go before us," in order to replace the absent Moses, "who brought us up out of the land of Egypt" (compare the end of v. 4; also note v.

100

7). So perhaps the golden calf is not intended as an artistic representation of Yahweh, but as a new leader for the people, one to take the place of Moses to conduct Israel on its way as ordained by Yahweh. Fretheim's observation that the calf was intended as "an image of the messenger of God" (281) is well taken. Clouding the issue still more is Yahweh's quick statement pointing out that the people have "worshiped" the image and have "sacrificed to it," something they never did to Moses (v. 8). From God's point of view, more is involved than simply a choice of a new leader on the part of a people dissatisfied with Moses. God's own person has been violated.

The final sentence of verse 6 also reveals that something is amiss. Not only did the people sacrifice and consume a meal, but they "rose up to revel." The verb used here, *tsahak*, literally means "to laugh" and is the basis of the wordplay in Genesis 17:17–19 (compare Gen. 18:12–15; 21:1–6) that offers an explanation for the name Isaac. The word is translated "jesting" in the story of Lot and the men of Sodom (Gen. 19:14), and "made sport" (RSV) or "performed" (NRSV) in the story of Samson's death in Judges 16:25. In both texts the word has sinister connotations. While laughter may be innocent at times, that "Moses saw that the people were running wild" (v. 25) is an ominous detail. Certainly this is no attitude to accompany the worship of the God of Israel.

> "It is Genesis 3 all over again. The garden scene becomes a tangled mess. Harmony turns to dissonance, rest to disturbance, preparedness to confusion, and the future with God becomes a highly uncertain matter." —Terence E. Fretheim, *Exodus*, Interpretation, 279.

God's Response

Yahweh's initial reaction to this terrible act of sinfulness is narrated in verses 7–14. Yahweh issues two commands to Moses which are consistent with each other but quite different in their implications: "Go down at once!" (v. 7), and "Let me alone" (v. 10). By means of the first of these commands Yahweh clarifies that the punishment for this terrible offense will be mediated through Moses. Just as Moses was cast in the role of Yahweh's agent in saving Israel at the Red Sea, so Moses will be God's instrument in the judgment of Israel. It is significant that Yahweh refers to Israel as "your people" and contrasts Moses' role as savior ("whom you brought up out of the land of Egypt") with the people's present perversity ("they have been quick to turn aside from the way that I commanded them," vv. 7–8).

Yahweh's second command to Moses is more intriguing and un-expected: "Now let me alone . . ." Perhaps Yahweh seeks solitude so as to permit the anger against the people to rage unchallenged. Yah-weh apparently fears (!) Moses will react by pleading on behalf of the people for God's mercy (vv. 11–14). But even in a seething rage, Yahweh makes a sharp distinction (v. 10) between the divine attitude toward the people (". . . that I may consume them") and toward Moses ("of you I will make a great nation," a promise that echoes the same commitment made to Abraham in Gen. 12:2). Yahweh is furi-ous and the people (so it would seem) are about to be destroyed, but God's plans for Israel have not been shattered. As the promise was once vested in a single individual in a previous generation, so it will be again. Moses is to be the new Abraham.

But Moses has a better idea than Yahweh. That fact is striking not just because it cuts against the grain of some of our notions about God's sovereignty and omniscience, but also because it reveals an as-tonishing portrait of Moses' self-under-standing. Most of us would be flattered that we had been singled out by God to be the sole repository of hopes for hu-mankind. But Moses has no need to feed a hungry ego. He deflects God's proposal that he be the new Abraham in favor of a plea that God show mercy on Israel. Yahweh can save the nation once again, this time not from Pharaoh, but from its own sinfulness.

> "The boldness of his reply indicates some-thing of the nature of the relationship be-tween God and Moses. God has so entered into this relationship that such dia-logue is invited, indeed welcomed: *God is not the only one who has something im-portant to say.*" —Terence E. Fretheim, *Ex-odus*, Interpretation 285.

Moses' appeal to Yahweh comprises three lines of approach:

1. Initially, Moses resorts to a logical argument (v. 11). For Yah-weh to lead the people to safety, and now turn on them to destroy them, would be a contradiction that would portray Yahweh as un-reasonable and quixotic. Note how Yahweh's earlier reference to "your [that is, Moses'] people" (v. 7) is now turned back against Yah-weh to deter him from his intended course of action. "Why does your wrath burn hot against *your* people . . .?" Moses asks Yahweh. Surely, for Yahweh to do away with his own nation is illogical!

2. A second line of approach (v. 12) speaks to Yahweh's reputation among the nations. Pharaoh had not long before led his army out into the countryside to decimate the fleeing Israelite slaves, a venture that had proved disastrous for the Egyptians. Imagine the glee they

would feel when the news got back to Memphis that Yahweh had done Pharaoh's work for him by wiping out the Israelites! Yahweh would appear to the Egyptians, and to others as well, as an especially evil God—more a demon than a deity. Surely Yahweh did not want that kind of reputation!

3. Finally (v. 13), as he did by invoking the phrase "your people," Moses again uses Yahweh's own words in an effort to win clemency for the people. "I will make of you a great nation," Yahweh had promised Moses (v. 10), but Moses reminds God that this promise has been made before. Wouldn't the better part of wisdom be to exercise mercy? Instead of wiping the slate clean and going all the way back to the state of affairs that existed during the time of "Abraham, Isaac, and Israel," couldn't Yahweh reconsider? Yes, Moses would have been gratified to know that Yahweh had enough confidence to make him a new Abraham, but what a waste of those long, toil-filled generations in Egypt! What a waste of this naive, if sinful, generation!

Lodged in the heart of these converging appeals is the essence of Moses' hope: "Turn from your fierce wrath; change your mind and do not bring disaster on your people" (v. 12).

Given Yahweh's basic commitment to mercy and to the redemption of the people (note, for example, Ex. 6:2–8), Yahweh cannot resist the force of Moses' words, for to do so would be a violation of Yahweh's own nature.

> "We get the picture of this great hero trying to pull God to his people and trying to pull his people to God. Moses: trying to pull heaven and earth together with his bare hands. We react with equal amazement: that Moses would stay faithful to such a people and that God would forgive and save us!" —H. Stephen Shoemaker, *God-Stories: New Narratives from Sacred Texts* (Valley Forge, Pa.: Judson Press, 1998), 84.

(Compare, for example, Yahweh's inner struggle with the issues of judgment and mercy in Hos. 11:1–9.) And so this section of the narrative ends on a note of grace: "And Yahweh changed his mind about the disaster that he planned to bring upon his people." No wonder Yahweh initially wanted Moses to "let me alone."

(For other biblical texts in which a human appeal apparently changes the intention of God or of Jesus, one may note Gen. 18:22–23; Amos 7:1–6; and Mark 7:24–30 [especially vv. 28–29]. The mysterious power of prayer includes the wondrous reality that God actually listens to us and responds to our needs.)

The Punishment of the People

As Childs notes in his discussion of Exodus 32:7–14 (568), "It [the text] epitomizes the essential paradox of the Hebrew faith: God is 'merciful and gracious . . . but will not clear the guilty'" (Ex. 34:7).

Although Moses did not comply with God's second command to "leave me alone," he does comply with the first, to "go down" (but not "at once"). Verses 15–20 describe his descent down the mountain and what occurs when he reaches the valley below. Moses is carrying the tablets of the Ten Commandments (note the detailed description of them in vv. 15–16). As he approaches the Israelite camp, he and Joshua hear the "noise of the people." Joshua is alarmed, thinking that it is the sound of fighting, and implies his fear that in Moses' absence, someone has attacked the Israelite encampment. Moses, who appears to quote an old unknown proverb or song, insists that the sound is not that of warriors but of merrymakers. The NRSV's "it is the sound of revelers that I hear" catches the spirit of the Hebrew, which literally reads "it is the sound of songs that I hear." The translation of the Hebrew Old Testament into Greek, the so-called Septuagint, produced about 200 B.C., also catches the spirit of the text. It renders the last line of verse 18: "I hear the voice of them that begin with wine." The party is in full swing as Moses comes close enough to see the golden calf and the people dancing (v. 19).

Regardless of what Yahweh intends for punishment, Moses has his own punishment of the people in mind. In one of the most dramatic scenes in the Old Testament, Moses throws down the tablets of the law, shattering them. Then, in a climax of rage, he has the golden calf burned (and, it would seem, melted down), the golden metal pulverized and then thrown into the drinking water (presum-

Key Terms

anthropomorphic Describing the divine with human characteristics. The gods portrayed in Greco-Roman mythology are extremely anthropomorphic.

Septuagint The Greek translation of the Old Testament, which was the Bible of the early church. It is often referred to by the Roman numerals LXX.

Why make the people drink the potion of the powdered calf?

Perhaps in the background of this scene is an understanding similar to that of Numbers 5:11–31. There, a suspected unfaithful wife must drink a potion made from the dust of the tabernacle floor, while swearing an oath. If she is guilty, she will become ill. If innocent, she will be spared. See J. Gerald Janzen, *Exodus,* Westminster Bible Companion, 237.

ably this is water contained in jars and leather bags, since there is no natural body of water at Horeb/Sinai), which the Israelites are forced to drink.

Aaron

Moses then confronts his older brother in a section of the text (vv. 21–24) that is a masterpiece in its portrayal of psychological rationalization. In response to Moses' question (v. 21), which really means, "Why did you show no backbone in the face of the sinful insistence of the people?" Aaron attempts to pass the buck. "Don't be mad at me," he says in effect. "You know how evil these people can be." Then Aaron quotes the harsh demand of the people almost exactly as it had been made to him (compare v. 23 with v. 1). "What's a poor fellow like me to do?" Aaron seems to be saying. "I had no choice. They made me do it."

Aaron's final statement deserves to be quoted directly. With only a passing reference to the fact that he asked for the people's gold (compare v. 24 with v. 2), he concludes, "I threw it [their gold] into the fire and out came this calf!" Aaron's words seem to be saying that the sin happened almost automatically, or as if by magic. He didn't make the calf; it just happened!

(Notice the similarities in this conversation between Moses and Aaron and that involving Yahweh, Adam, and Eve in Gen. 3:8–13.)

So Aaron joins the ranks of a number of important biblical figures who, though otherwise faithful, exhibit a moment of spiritual cowardice when confronted with great danger (note the story of Peter's denial in Matt. 26:69–75). In a sense, it is that frailty which makes many modern readers of the Bible—we who have also suffered moments of spiritual timidity—relate more easily to Aaron than to the stalwart Moses.

Nevertheless, Aaron is held up for ridicule as the text moves forward to describe the next phase in the punishment of the people (vv. 25–29). Not only had Aaron made the golden calf, but he was

> Perhaps Aaron "believed with the rest of mankind that a God in the hand is worth two in the bush." —Frederick Buechner, *Peculiar Treasures: A Biblical Who's Who* (San Francisco: Harper & Row, 1979), 2.

responsible for the disrespectful behavior of the people (v. 25). The Hebrew term used to describe the conduct of the Israelites is somewhat obscure, but seems to mean "to turn loose." The NRSV's "running wild" is wonderfully evocative of the scene that met Moses' eyes. Shocked by this orgy, Moses stands at the gate of the camp—a location comparable to the courthouse square in a typical small American town (note the discussion of the Ninth Commandment in unit 8)—and issues a challenge. All who are still loyal to Yahweh must demonstrate their commitment by standing next to Moses. This is the first time individual Israelites have been called upon to confess their faithfulness, although the nation as a whole has done so previously (19:8, 24:3). The scene previews a similar moment in the life of the nation which will occur under the leadership of Joshua (Josh. 24:15).

The Killing by the Levites

The men of the tribe of Levi are the only Israelites who respond to Moses' summons. They are directed to go through the camp and kill all of their compatriots who are still apostate, even their own relatives and friends. They do so at terrible cost. Some three thousand people are slaughtered, but the Levites as a group win an important distinction for themselves. They gain ordination "to the service of Yahweh" (v. 29), an apparent reference to the priestly status that Levites will enjoy from this time onward.

Verses 25–29 raise some difficult questions. Moses has already punished the people by forcing them to drink water laced with gold dust from the destroyed image, and Yahweh will presently unfold a plan for an additional punishment in store in the form of a plague (vv. 34–35). What is the purpose of this seemingly unnecessary and "extra" punishment? Also, since the Levites did not kill *all* the backsliding Israelites, or Moses would have had no one left to lead but the Levites themselves, how did the Levites decide who to kill and who to allow to live? Furthermore, although three thousand is a large number, if the total number of the people is still in excess of six hundred thousand (Ex. 12:37), the dead represent a small minority. The impression that only a few Israelites were guilty of sin is at variance with the whole sense of 32:1–35.

Because of these features in the text and because of the unusual prominence here of the Levites, some scholars have raised the possibility that 32:25–29 was an insertion. In what is otherwise a rather straightforward narrative, perhaps this little story was placed there in order to enhance the prestige of the Levites, the priestly class within

Israel who play a central role in the life of the nation until the destruction of Jerusalem by the Romans in A.D. 70. If verses 25–29 were absent, one would read from verse 24 to verse 30 without a sense that something is missing.

Having been instrumental now in punishing the people twice, Moses turns to Yahweh in order to intercede for them (vv. 30–34). In so doing, Moses is once more fulfilling his role as the one who mediates between Yahweh and the people. Not only do the people need Moses to represent them to Yahweh, but Yahweh is just as dependent upon Moses to communicate to the people. Verse 14 has already indicated that any plans on Yahweh's part to annihilate Israel have been abandoned, and undoubtedly Moses now leans on this promise.

Moses Intercedes for the People

Verse 32 is one of the most remarkable in the book of Exodus. In effect, Moses challenges Yahweh to live up to a reputation for mercy by presenting Yahweh with two alternative courses of action. "If you will only forgive their sin—" is one half of an "if . . ., then . . ." sentence whose "then" section is left unstated for emphasis. "If you will only forgive their sin, *then do so!*" is the way the entire sentence would run. This is the first of Yahweh's possible choices. The second is

> "Now the one-time shepherd's heart was breaking over his new flock." —H. L. Ellison, *Exodus,* Daily Study Bible (Philadelphia: Westminster Press, 1982), 174.

terrifying: "If you will not forgive their sin, then destroy me along with the people" is the essential meaning of the final part of the verse. Moses must have been tempted to claim the promise extended to him in verse 10: namely, that after Yahweh had "consumed" the people, the promise made to Abraham would now be vested in Moses. If Yahweh could not forgive Israel, then Moses wants nothing to do with such a God!

(Incidentally, the "book" to which Moses refers in v. 32 is apparently a listing of the members of the saved community, and may be compared to similar references in Ps. 69:28 and Dan. 12:1. Verse 33 should be read as a declaration of the incompatibility of sinfulness and faithfulness on the part of people—not a suggestion that God won't forgive sinners.)

Yahweh responds to Moses' astonishing courage by reaffirming the promise of Exodus 23:23: "My angel shall go in front of you" (32:34). Yet sin is too serious a matter to be ignored. Yahweh reserves a time for an appropriate punishment, an intention that is fulfilled by the plague of verse 35. This brief notation, interestingly, provides no information about the duration of the plague or about the number of its casualties—almost certainly a way to downplay its seriousness.

The Irony of Their Idolatry

In the beginning of the discussion of Exodus, we noted the presence of irony as a literary device in the text (see unit 1). Of all the instances of irony in Exodus, surely 32:1–35 is the most glaring, not in literary terms, but in theological. Hardly has Yahweh saved the people by allowing them to cross safely through the Red Sea, hardly has the covenant been renewed with them, until they reject Yahweh, their unseen friend, in favor of a glittering image. In fact, Moses is *still* on the mountain engaged in conversation with Yahweh—still receiving Yahweh's instruction on their behalf—when the people fall away. They turn from an earlier worshipful commitment (19:8, 24:3) to an orgiastic frenzy of eating, drinking, and merriment (32:6, 25). The community of faith has become a community of sin.

Want to Know More?

About the Septuagint? See Celia Brewer Marshall, *A Guide through the Old Testament* (Louisville, Ky.: Westminster John Knox Press, 1989), 20; J. Alberto Soggin, *Introduction to the Old Testament*, 3d ed., Old Testament Library (Louisville, Ky.: Westminster John Knox Press, 1989), 23–26.

About Levites? See Paul J. Achtemeier, ed., *Harper's Bible Dictionary* (San Francisco: Harper & Row, 1985), 557–58; Horst Dietrich Preuss, *Old Testament Theology*, vol. 2, Old Testament Library (Louisville, Ky.: Westminster John Knox Press, 1996), 52–62.

There is little wonder that the story of the golden calf has loomed large in the consciousness of many men and women of faith. Ezekiel 20:8, Acts 7:40–42 (Ex. 32:1 is quoted almost verbatim in 7:40), and 1 Corinthians 10:7 (which quotes Ex. 32:6) are all texts that recall this terrible moment of Israel's sinfulness. In each case (although from different perspectives), the later passages cite the golden calf incident as an example of how God's people are not to live or act. The references remind the community of faith to maintain a life of faithfulness to God, even when God *appears* distant and uninvolved. As Exodus 32 makes quite clear, such a state of affairs is an appearance only—and never a reality!

Still God's People

At least two enduring words of grace may be spoken about the tale of the golden calf. The first is that the courage and faithfulness of Moses provides an example of commitment that all God's people may emulate. Moses is not only obedient to God; he is willing to give up his own salvation for the sake of the people. Small wonder that many a Christian preacher has described Moses as a Christlike figure.

The second word of grace that arises out of Exodus 32 has to do with God's willingness to forgive. The reality that divine grace does not come easily or cheaply is quite dramatically illustrated by Yahweh's reaction to the people's sin in 32:10: Yahweh's initial impulse is to obliterate these treacherous people entirely. But Yahweh's words also reveal a struggle within to suppress a gentler nature. God commands Moses to leave so that the divine wrath will not be impeded. But Moses coaxes Yahweh to do that which Yahweh really wants to do—forgive the people. And so in verse 14, Yahweh "changed his mind."

The story of this fugitive people cannot end at 32:35. The narrative must go on, and Israel must go on—a people and their God bound inseparably together. The climactic event of the book of Exodus is not Israel's worship of the golden calf but Yahweh's restoration of their covenant relationship (chap. 34).

? Questions for Reflection

1. We too often take time for granted, but forty days and forty nights can be a long time, and much can change. What has changed in the past forty days (in the world at large and in your life)?

2. This passage is a shining example of the instability of the faithfulness of the Israelites. What tempts you to be unstable in your commitment to God? (Here is another way to think about this question: Aaron came up with some good rationalizations for making the golden calf. What are some of the rationalizations you use?)

3. In one of the most interesting passages in all of scripture, God and Moses argue and talk out some decisions. The boldness of Moses

can be unnerving, but Moses had an enviable intimacy with God. What are ways you can draw close to God? What are things about which you would argue with God?

4. The last verses of this passage speak about God blotting out names from a book. This is a drastic statement of judgment. How do you come to terms with the notion of God's judgment?

The Covenant Restored

Early in the discussion, the element of gospel in the book of Exodus was cited (see the Introduction). Nowhere is the good news of God's saving grace more evident than in the relationship between Exodus 32, with its sordid tale of the golden calf, and Exodus 34, the narrative of Yahweh's gracious restoration of the covenant with the chosen people. A number of scholars point to this important connection, some even suggesting a literary unity for Exodus 32–34 which is older than the present location of these chapters in the book of Exodus. However that may be, these chapters certainly constitute an important subsection within the book and contain a compelling declaration about human sin and divine forgiveness.

Chapter 33

Exodus 32 ends on a note of judgment. Although Yahweh has "changed his mind" (32:14) about completely destroying this sinful people (note v. 10), Moses is told that the sin of the golden calf will not be ignored (32:34) and a plague is sent upon the people (32:35). That somber mood of judgment continues into Exodus 33. Although Yahweh repeats the promise to "send an angel" to protect the people in their journey toward the Land of Promise (33:2; compare 32:34), there is the insistence that "I will not go up among you" (33:3). The reason: Yahweh would destroy the people because they are "stiff-necked" (notice how v. 5 repeats the judgment of v. 3), and because in their sinful condition they could not abide God's holiness. In contrition over their sin, the people remove their ornaments.

After a brief section that describes the "tent of meeting" where

Moses regularly engages Yahweh in conversation (33:7–11), Moses asks for further guidance. "Whom will you send with me?" (33:12) he wants to know, perhaps a reference to the angel of 32:34 and 33:2—who, incidentally, is never heard from again. Also, "show me your ways," Moses demands (33:13) in order that "I may know you" (that is, "know what you're up to") and "find favor in your sight" ("do the job correctly that you have called me to do"). Moses also reminds Yahweh, as he did earlier (32:11), that Israel is "your people" (33:13).

Astonishingly, Yahweh does an abrupt about-face and promises to accompany Moses personally along the way. "My presence will go with you," Yahweh affirms, "and I will give you rest." Yahweh then seals this promise by means of two significant actions. First (33:19), the divine name, Yahweh, is affirmed, as in Exodus 3:15 and 6:2. This is more than an act of self-identification, more than a manner of saying, "I am still the same God you have been dealing with all along." It is an act of self-revelation, as were the earlier pronouncements (see unit 2).

The second thing Yahweh does (33:21–23) is appear to Moses in physical form. This is quite unexpected, for verses 20 and 23 are clear that no one, not even Moses, may look God in the face and live. (Of course, vv. 20 and 23 contradict 33:11, where Yahweh and Moses converse "face to face, as one speaks to a friend.") So Moses is shown Yahweh's "glory" and "back," and thereby the good faith of Yahweh's promises is demonstrated.

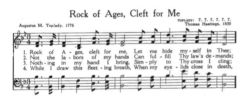

Rock of Ages, Cleft for Me

A powerful image drawn from Exodus 33:22

In summary, Exodus 33 describes important activity by both Moses and Yahweh. Moses successfully appeals for Yahweh's grace, thereby fulfilling once again his task as Israel's mediator with God. Yahweh responds by promising continued guidance to Moses and the people.

A Covenant Again

As a climactic means to affirm that the sin of the golden calf will not prove fatal to Israel's life before God, Exodus 34 describes a renewal of the covenant made at Horeb/Sinai (which, as noted earlier, was itself a renewal of the covenant made with Abraham in Genesis 15 and 17). Initially, Yahweh directs Moses to "cut two tablets of stone like the former ones" (34:1), that is, like the ones Moses shattered in his anger over the incident of the golden calf (32:19). That Moses now is to produce these new tablets, whereas Yahweh had provided the original pair, may be symbolic of Moses' role in the process. As Moses was instrumental in expressing God's anger over the golden calf, now he is instrumental in restoring the people to their former state of grace with God. Moses' role in the production of the new tablets is limited to their preparation, for Yahweh will write the words of the law upon the tablets, "the [same] words that were on the former tablets, which you broke." (But note 34:27, where Yahweh dictates the words to Moses, which Moses then writes upon the tablets.) It is quite clear from all of this that we should expect that the basis of the renewed covenant will be the same as the covenant described in Exodus 19–20: the Ten Commandments.

Moses meets Yahweh under conditions similar to those in 19:12–13, 21–23, except that some of the former details are not provided, such as the earthquake, thunder and lightning, and so on. The most notable difference is the people's entirely passive role, unlike their former promises to obey what Yahweh has commanded (19:8, 24:3). In the narrative of Exodus 34, Moses alone accepts the renewed covenant on behalf of the people, another sign of the emphasis within this text on his role as mediator. This also seems to be an important statement of God's grace, implying that God's mercy is not dependent upon the activity of the people, but is given for its own sake. Yahweh descends in a cloud at the top of the mountain to declare the name: Yahweh (34:5).

A Song of God

Yahweh utilizes the divine name as the theme for a song or poem that is recited in Moses' presence: "Yahweh, Yahweh, a God merciful and gracious . . ." (34:6–7). The statement is presented here as a self-affirmation by Yahweh, but its many other occurrences in the Old Testament (compare Num. 14:18; Neh. 9:17; Ps. 86:15; Jonah 4:2) prove that it became important to Israel's faith and understanding of Yahweh. Arguably, this is as close as the Old Testament comes to a concrete definition of God. In that regard, notice that the words used to describe God are all *adjectives* such as "merciful" or "gracious" (a way of saying "God is *similar to* certain qualities in human beings") and *verbs* such as "keeping," "forgiving," or "visiting" (a way of insisting that one encounters God because one has encountered what God is *doing*). At no place in this confession is God defined with a *noun*, presumably because any attempt at such a definition must end in failure. (The nearest the Old Testament comes to such a definition is in the mysterious "I am that I am" of Ex. 3:14.) Perhaps most interesting is this confessional statement's framing of Yahweh as a God who is forgiving and yet holds the people accountable for their sins.

> "The Hebrew word that 'forgiving' translates here is revealing. It means . . . 'bearing with' or 'putting up with.' But 'bearing with' comes at the cost of pain and sorrow to the one who bears, so, in a real sense, the forgiver is the one who bears the sin of the forgiven." —J. Gerald Janzen, *Exodus*, Westminster Bible Companion, 255.

A Plea for the People

Moses' response to this self-affirmation by God is to bow and worship (34:8–9). He repeats his plea for Yahweh to forgive the people for their sin in the orgy of the golden calf. In important ways the prayer of 34:9 repeats Moses' plea for mercy in 33:12–13, especially since both petitions are based on Moses' good standing in Yahweh's heart. If 34:9 has a special emphasis, it is found perhaps in Moses' reference once more to Israel's posture of obstinacy before God, that they are a "stiff-necked people." Moses asks God to forgive the people not because they are radically changed

> **Who's being stubborn now?**
>
> "The word for 'stiff' has the same root as one of the words for Pharaoh's 'hard heart.'" —Terence E. Fretheim, *Exodus*, Interpretation, 304.

(although note their contrition in 33:4–6), but because Yahweh has promised that they will be his special people. Thus Moses concludes his prayer with an appeal to Yahweh's own previously expressed commitment to the nation: ". . . and take us for your inheritance."

Yahweh responds in a manner consistent with the description of verses 6–7. Yahweh promises to restore the covenant and perform such wonderful things in Israel's life that they cannot be compared with the experience of any other people (34:10). In these few lines of text, Yahweh renews the promise that not only will Israel be a special people, but that God will lead them safely into their own land, a promise spelled out in more detail in 34:11.

The Giving of the Law

What follows next is puzzling. The basis for this renewed covenant is to be the same as before, namely the Ten Commandments, which will be rewritten by Yahweh upon the tablets of stone that Moses provided (34:1), an identification that is affirmed again in the text (34:28). But what the reader discovers instead is not the Ten Commandments of Exodus 20:1–17, but a different set of laws, only some of which are similar to the Ten Commandments, and whose total does not even number ten (although the method of enumerating them is somewhat arbitrary).

Another observation concerns their ritualistic nature. None of these laws deals with the "everyday" affairs among the Israelites (as do the Fifth through Tenth Commandments, Ex. 20:12–17). As Fretheim suggests (309), this may be because Israel's sin involving the golden calf was ritualistic in nature.

Exodus 34:11–16

If this passage is intended to be one of the laws of the renewed covenant, it is cast in a very unusual formula, quite unlike any of the others. This law begins by promising that the people whom the Israelites will meet in the Land of Promise will be subdued by divine power (v.11). In return, the Israelites will not enter into treaty obligations with them, nor worship at their shrines (which are to be destroyed), nor intermarry with them. On the surface, the prohibitions appear to be political or social, but in reality they are theological. These alien people are not holy as Israel is holy. To have any attitude toward them other than hostility violates God's holiness. The affirmation in verse 14 that Yahweh is a jealous/zealous God makes that clear. Although the language is similar to that of the Second Commandment (note the discussion in unit 7 of "jealous" and "zealous"), in its larger conception, 34:11–16 resonates more with the First Commandment, 20:3.

Exodus 34:17

In a brief recapitulation of 20:4, the prohibition that begins the Second Commandment, this law forbids idols.

Exodus 34:18

This passage is the first of several references to the three great annual festivals of ancient Israel: Passover/Unleavened Bread in the spring, Weeks (later called Pentecost) also in the spring, and Ingathering or Booths (also called Tabernacles) in the autumn (compare Deut. 16:1–17). Oddly, although 34:18 is a command to observe Pentecost/Unleavened Bread, the statements about the other two festivals do not appear until 34:22 (Weeks and Ingathering, respectively), after a statement regarding Sabbath observance (34:21). In addition, the discussion of the festivals seems to have become splintered, with fragments dislodged throughout the verses (34:18–26). The final sentence of verse 20 ("No one shall appear before me empty-handed) is attached to a commandment regarding the firstborn (more about this below), whereas in 23:15 the same sentence is tied to the observance of Passover/Unleavened Bread. Also, though detached in the text, verses 25 and 26 seem to be related to the commands concerning Passover/Unleavened Bread and Ingathering (vv. 18 and 22).

Exodus 34:19–20

This statement about the dedication of all the firstborn is similar to 13:11–16, where that declaration is connected to the observance of Passover. However, the practice of sacrificing firstborn animals (substitutes could be obtained for human children and valuable livestock) does not appear to have become a standard feature of Israelite Passover observance, with the exception of the sacrifice of the Passover lamb (note Deut. 16:1–8).

Exodus 34:21

This is an abbreviated form of the Fourth Commandment found in 20:8–11 (compare Deut. 5:12–15).

Exodus 34:22–26

See the comments above concerning 34:18. A summary statement about the three great annual festivals is found in 34:23–24. Interestingly, 34:24 ties the faithful keeping of the three festivals to Yahweh's promise to expel all other nations from the Land of Promise, as found in 34:11. The last sentence of 34:26, the prohibition against boiling a kid in its mother's milk, seems unrelated to the first part of the verse, but the same juxtaposition is found in 23:19.

This unusual mixture of legal requirements has caused many scholars to view Exodus 34 as the end product of a long and complex literary history. They see here the work of many writers who did not always share the same understanding of the significance of the passage. In one view, Exodus 34 initially described how Yahweh made the original covenant with Israel; it was similar or identical to Exodus 19–20, and at a later time (and by different hands) the text was reshaped to describe a *renewal* of the covenant of Exodus 19–20. That 34:11–26 is bracketed with the statements "I hereby make a covenant" (v. 10) and "I have made a covenant with you and with Israel" (v. 27) would seem to support this view.

The Covenant Reaffirmed

In its present form, 34:1–35 is intended to describe a renewal of the covenant made at Horeb/Sinai. That covenant was broken by a sinful people in their worship of the golden calf but now is restored by a merciful God. So in this sense, 34:27–28 provides a summary of this story of covenant renewal. Moses writes upon the tablets, which he brought up the mountain, the words that Yahweh dictates, the words that are to seal the reaffirmed covenant. For "forty days and forty nights," that is, for a very long time, Moses is with Yahweh on the mountain engaged in engraving, during which time he has nothing to eat or drink (compare Elijah's experience in 1 Kings 19:4–8—which, incidentally, culminates in an appearance of Yahweh to the prophet that is clearly written with Ex. 33:17–23 in mind—and that of Jesus in Matt. 4:2). The final sentence of verse 28 affirms that the words which Moses etched on the new tablets are the same as those of Exodus 20:3–17, the Ten Commandments (note 34:1).

A Glowing Face

There is a final, fascinating story in this narrative of covenant renewal, that of Moses and his shining face, 34:29–35. It is a strange and incomprehensible story, but one whose significance is clear. The focus of the passage is on Moses and his unique role as the mediator between Yahweh and Yahweh's people, illustrated by the frequent references to Moses' speaking either to the people (vv. 31 [twice], 32, 33, 34) or to Yahweh (vv. 34, 35). The most unusual feature of the passage is the statement that, unknown to Moses, "the skin of his face shone" (vv. 29, 30), a reflected glow that resulted from his frequent proximity to Yahweh and Yahweh's glory. The people might mistake this glow for a sign that Moses himself had become divine (compare the story of Paul and Barnabas in Acts 14:11–18) and make a sinful error similar to that of the golden calf incident by falling down to worship Moses. In order to avoid this calamity, Moses covered his face with a veil. He removed it only when he spoke to Yahweh (v. 34) or to the people on Yahweh's behalf (v. 35), to emphasize that his radiance was merely a reflection of the radiance of Yahweh. Otherwise, he continued to use the veil to shield his glowing face (compare the reference to the shining presence of Jesus in Mark 9:3).

> "Moses' shining face is the vision of the face of God which is available to the community of faith." —Terence E. Fretheim, *Exodus*, Interpretation, 311.

There is an interesting historical footnote to this passage. The Hebrew verb that is translated "shone" or "shining" in verses 29, 30, and 35 literally means something like "to send out rays." In the noun form, the meaning is "horn"; in Ezekiel 27:15 it refers to elephant tusks and in 1 Samuel 16:1 to the horn of an ox, used as a flask for oil. Not surprisingly, the Vulgate, a translation of the Bible from the fourth century A.D. associated with Jerome, mistook the passage and described how Moses had "horns." Thereafter, it became traditional for Moses to appear with horns in stained-glass windows, paintings, and other artistic representations, including Michelangelo's great statue of Moses in Rome.

The horns of Moses

The Message of Exodus

In Exodus 34 the reader finds the climax of the entire book of Exodus. To be sure, other material lies ahead (Exodus 35–40), mostly having to do with the construction of the Tabernacle, the manufacture of the ark of the covenant, the nature of the vestments for the priests, and other details of Israel's life of worship. But that information is something of an afterglow, at least in theological terms. The basic message of the book has been proclaimed: God has called and saved Israel to be a special people, for the benefit of all humankind. Although this special relationship and thus God's purposes have been threatened by the people's sin, both Israel and humankind will ultimately be judged not only by God's justice but also by

> "It is *as creator* that God makes these moves on Israel's behalf; this is God's way with the world generally." —Terence E. Fretheim, *Exodus,* Interpretation, 305.

God's mercy. Indeed, Exodus makes clear that when divine justice and divine mercy collide, divine mercy will prevail (note especially in this regard Hosea's summary of Israel's exodus experience in Hos. 11:1–9).

In one important sense Exodus can be regarded as a story about Yahweh, a narrative of an incomprehensible Mystery who comes out of a desert bush to reclaim a people apparently long forgotten. A Mystery who bonds with that people in love and continues to hold them close, in spite of their wriggling to be free and their complaint that they are underprotected. A Mystery who shields the people and sends them safely on their way to a land already prepared.

On another level, Exodus is a biography of the man Moses, or at least a biography of the first 80 or so years of his 120-year life. We follow the activities of this man from his watery cradle through the most momentous events of his life—all of his life, actually, except for his final years in the desert until his death and burial on the plains of Moab (Deut. 34:1–12).

On yet another level, Exodus is the story of the rebirth of a nation, a nation that sprang miraculously from its elderly parents, Abraham and Sarah, flourished for a period in both Canaan and Egypt, and then all but disappeared under the cruel oppression of Pharaoh's rule. That a nation could be resurrected from the dustbin of history in so remarkable a fashion might be regarded as evidence that, although we may be shaped by our experiences of the past, we are not necessarily imprisoned by them.

Actually, however, Exodus is a story about all three—about Yahweh, Moses, and Israel and how they interact with, and relate to, each other. Ultimately, Exodus is a story about all humankind. If Yahweh is the means by which Israel is saved, then Israel becomes the means by which Yahweh becomes known to the nations of the world. If Yahweh needs Moses to reveal the divine will to Israel, Israel needs Moses to represent it before the powerful God of justice and love—and Moses, for his part, needs both Yahweh and Israel, to fulfill his role as the most important mediator in the life of Israel-of-old.

Want to Know More?

About the cleft in the rock incident? See Terence E. Fretheim, *Exodus*, Interpretation (Louisville, Ky.: John Knox Press, 1991), 299–301.

About what happens to Moses later? See Numbers 13–32 and Deuteronomy 34; see also John Van Seters, *The Life of Moses: The Yahwist as Historian in Exodus–Numbers* (Louisville, Ky.: Westminster John Knox Press, 1994), 361–468.

Therefore, of the many enduring lessons of Exodus, none is more crucial than this: A God of justice and love has met creation at the point of its deepest need—the weakness and sin of humankind. While not renouncing justice, this God responded by identifying with this people and by reaching out to them in love to rescue them from themselves and from all those powers that threaten them. If Moses was the means by which God's grace met the people once before, Christians find God's final and enduring mediator in Jesus Christ. Jesus is the new Moses for whom the old Moses prepared the way. And so we *all* cross the Red Sea. We *all* worship the golden calf. We *all* are invited to receive the renewed covenant—not because we deserve it, but because it is God's gracious gift to a sinful world.

❓ Questions for Reflection

1. This passage begins with the remaking of the tablets, an image of the renewing of God's covenant with the Israelites. What are some images you could use to describe to a child the concept of mending something that was broken?

2. After meeting God face to face, Moses' face shone. If the church is a vibrant example of the presence of God, what are ways we can show God's presence?

3. What are ways the themes of creation, promise, and continuity and discontinuity have been presented in the ten passages from the book of Exodus (units 1–10)?

4. Exodus may be described as the intertwining of the stories of Moses and God. The story of Exodus comes alive when we find ourselves within it. Where are the intersections of your life within Exodus?

Bibliography

Charlesworth, James H., ed. *The Old Testament Pseudepigrapha.* Volume 2. Garden City, N.J.: Doubleday & Co., 1985.

Childs, Brevard S. *The Book of Exodus.* The Old Testament Library. Philadelphia: Westminister Press, 1974.

Durham, John I. *Exodus.* Word Biblical Commentary. Waco, Tex.: Word Publishing, 1987.

Fretheim, Terence E. *Exodus.* Interpretation. Louisville, Ky.: John Knox Press, 1991.

Janzen, J. Gerald. *Exodus.* Westminster Bible Companion. Louisville, Ky.: Westminster John Knox Press, 1997.

McCarthy, Dennis J. *Treaty and Covenant.* Rome: Pontifical Biblical Institute, 1963, 1972.

Pritchard, James B., ed. *Ancient Near Eastern Texts Relating to the Old Testament.* Third edition with supplement. Princeton, N.J.: Princeton University Press, 1969.

Interpretation Bible Studies
Leader's Guide

Interpretation Bible Studies (IBS), for adults and older youth, are flexible, attractive, easy-to-use, and filled with solid information about the Bible. IBS helps Christians discover the guidance and power of the scriptures for living today. Perhaps you are leading a church school class, a midweek Bible study group, or a youth group meeting, or simply using this in your own personal study. Whatever the setting may be, we hope you find this *Leader's Guide* helpful. Since every context and group is different, this *Leader's Guide* does not presume to tell you how to structure Bible study for your situation. Instead, the *Leader's Guide* seeks to offer choices—a number of helpful suggestions for leading a successful Bible study using IBS.

> "The church that no longer hears the essential message of the Scriptures soon ceases to understand what it is for and is open to be captured by the dominant religious philosophy of the moment." —James D. Smart, *The Strange Silence of the Bible in the Church: A Study in Hermeneutics* (Philadelphia: Westminster Press, 1970), 10.

How Should I Teach IBS?

1. Explore the Format

There is a wealth of information in IBS, perhaps more than you can use in one session. In this case, more is better. IBS has been designed to give you a well-stocked buffet of content and teachable insights. Pick and choose what suits your group's needs. Perhaps you will want to split units into two or more sessions, or combine units into a single session. Perhaps you will decide to use only a portion of a

> "The more we bring to the Bible, the more we get from the Bible." —William Barclay, *A Beginner's Guide to the New Testament* (Louisville, Ky.: Westminster John Knox Press, 1995), vii.

unit and then move on to the next unit. *There is not a structured theme or teaching focus to each unit that must be followed for IBS to be used.* Rather, IBS offers the flexibility to adjust to whatever suits your context.

A recent survey of both professional and volunteer church educators revealed that their number one concern was that Bible study materials be teacher-friendly. IBS is, indeed teacher-friendly in two important ways. First, since IBS provides abundant content and a flexible design, teachers can shape the lessons creatively, responding to the needs of the group and employing a wide variety of teaching methods. Second, those who wish more specific suggestions for planning the sessions can find them at the Geneva Press web site on the Internet (**www.ppcpub.org**). Search under the keyword "Interpretation Bible Studies" to discover teaching suggestions for each IBS unit as well as helpful quotations, selections from Bible dictionaries and encyclopedias, and other teaching helps.

IBS is also not only teacher-friendly, it is also discussion-friendly. Given the opportunity, most adults and young people relish the chance to talk about the kind of issues raised in IBS. The secret, then, is to determine what works with your group, what will get them to talk. Several good methods for stimulating discussion are presented in this *Leader's Guide,* and once you learn your group, you can apply one of these methods and get the group discussing the Bible and its relevance in their lives.

The format of every IBS unit consists of several features:

a. Body of the Unit. This is the main content, consisting of interesting and informative commentary on the passage and scholarly insight into the biblical text and its significance for Christians today.

b. Sidebars. These are boxes that appear scattered throughout the body of the unit, with maps, photos, quotations, and intriguing ideas. Some sidebars can be identified quickly by a symbol, or icon, that helps the reader know what type of information can be found in that sidebar. There are icons for illustrations, key terms, pertinent quotes, and more.

c. Want to Know More? Each unit includes a "Want to Know

More?" section that guides learners who wish to dig deeper and consult other resources. If your church library does not have the resources mentioned, you can look up the information in other
standard Bible dictionaries, encyclopedias, and handbooks, or you
can find much of this information at the Geneva Press Web site (see
page 112).

d. Questions for Reflection. The unit ends with questions to
help the learners think more deeply about the biblical passage and
its pertinence for today. These ques-
tions are provided as examples only, and
teachers are encouraged both to develop
their own list of questions and to gather
questions from the group. These discussion questions do not usually have specific "correct" answers. Again, the

> "The trick is to make the Bible our book."
> —Duncan S. Ferguson, *Bible Basics:
> Mastering the Content of the Bible*
> (Louisville, Ky.: Westminster John Knox
> Press, 1995), 3.

flexibility of IBS allows you to use these questions at the end of the
group time, at the beginning, interspersed throughout, or not at all.

2. Select a Teaching Method

Here are ten suggestions. The format of IBS allows you to choose
what direction you will take as you plan to teach. Only you will
know how your lesson should best be designed for your group. Some
adult groups prefer the lecture method, while others prefer a high
level of free ranging discussion. Many youth groups like interaction,
activity, the use of music, and the chance to talk about their own experiences and feelings. Here is a list of a few possible approaches. Let your
own creativity add to the list!

a. Let's Talk about What We've Learned. In this approach,
all group members are requested to read the scripture passage and
the IBS unit before the group meets. Ask the group members to
make notes about the main issues, concerns, and questions they see
in the passage. When the group meets, these notes are collected,
shared, and discussed. This method depends, of course, on the
group's willingness to do some "homework."

b. What Do We Want and Need to Know? This approach
begins by having the whole group read the scripture passage together.

Then, drawing from your study of the IBS, you, as the teacher, write on a board or flip chart two lists:

(1) Things we should know to better understand this passage" (content information related to the passage, for example, historical insights about political contexts, geographical landmarks, economic nuances, etc.] and

(2) Four or five "important issues we should talk about regarding this passage" [with implications for today- how the issues in the biblical context continue into today, for example, issues of idolatry or fear]. Allow the group to add to either list, if they wish, and use the lists to lead into a time of learning, reflection, and discussion. This approach is suitable for those settings where there is little or no advanced preparation by the students.

> "Although small groups can meet for many purposes and draw upon many different resources, the one resource which has shaped the life of the Church more than any other throughout its long history has been the Bible." —Roberta Hestenes, *Using the Bible in Groups* (Philadelphia: Westminster Press, 1983), 14.

c. Hunting and Gathering. Start the unit by having the group read the scripture passage together. Then divide the group into smaller clusters (perhaps having as few as one person), each with a different assignment. Some clusters can discuss one or more of the "Questions for Reflection." Others can look up key terms or people in a Bible dictionary or track down other biblical references found in the body of the unit. After the small clusters have had time to complete their tasks, gather the entire group again and lead them through the study material, allowing each cluster to contribute what it learned.

d. From Question Mark to Exclamation Point. This approach begins with contemporary questions and then moves to the biblical content as a response to those questions. One way to do this is for you to ask the group, at the beginning of the class, a rephrased version of one or more of the "Questions for Reflection" at the end of the study unit. For example, one of the questions at the end of the unit on Exodus 3:1–4:17 in the IBS *Exodus* volume reads,

> Moses raised four protests, or objections, to God's call. Contemporary people also raise objections to God's call. In what ways are these similar to Moses' protests? In what ways are they different?

This question assumes familiarity with the biblical passage about

Moses, so the question would not work well before the group has explored the passage. However, try rephrasing this question as an opening exercise; for example:

> Here is a thought experiment: Let's assume that God, who called people in the Bible to do daring and risky things, still calls people today to tasks of faith and courage. In the Bible, God called Moses from a burning bush and called Isaiah in a moment of ecstatic worship in the Temple. How do you think God's call is experienced by people today? Where do you see evidence of people saying "yes" to God's call? When people say "no" or raise an objection to God's call, what reasons do they give (to themselves, to God)?

Posing this or a similar question at the beginning will generate discussion and raise important issues, and then it can lead the group into an exploration of the biblical passage as a resource for thinking even more deeply about these questions.

e. Let's Go to the Library.   From your church library, your pastor's library, or other sources, gather several good commentaries on the book of the Bible you are studying. Among the trustworthy commentaries are those in the Interpretation series (John Knox Press) and the Westminster Bible Companion series (Westminster John Knox Press). Divide your group into smaller clusters and give one commentary to each cluster (one or more of the clusters can be given the IBS volume instead of a full-length commentary). Ask each cluster to read the biblical passage you are studying and then to read the section of the commentary that covers that passage (if your group is large, you may want to make photocopies of the commentary material with proper permission, of course). The task of each cluster is to name the two or three most important insights they discover about the biblical passage by reading and talking together about the commentary material. When you reassemble the larger group to share these insights, your group will not only gain a variety of insights about the passage but also a sense that differing views of the same text are par for the course in biblical interpretation.

f. Working Creatively Together.   Begin with a creative group task, tied to the main thrust of the study. For example, if the study is on the Ten Commandments, a parable, or a psalm, have the group rewrite the Ten Commandments, the parable, or the psalm in contemporary language. If the passage is an epistle, have the group write a letter to their own congregation. Or if the study is a narrative, have the group role-play the characters in the story or write a page describing the story from the point of view of one of the characters. After completion of the task, read and discuss the biblical passage, asking for interpretations and applications from the group and tying in IBS material as it fits the flow of the discussion.

g. Singing Our Faith. Begin the session by singing (or reading) together a hymn that alludes to the biblical passage being studied (or to the theological themes in the passage). Most hymnals have an index of scriptural allusions. For example, if you are studying the unit from the IBS volume on Psalm 121, you can sing "I to the Hills Will Lift My Eyes," "Sing Praise to God, Who Reigns Above," or another hymn based on Psalm 121. Let the group reflect on the thoughts and feelings evoked by the hymn, then move to the biblical passage, allowing the biblical text and the IBS material to underscore, clarify, refine, and deepen the discussion stimulated by the hymn. If you are ambitious, you may ask the group to write a new hymn at the end of the study! [Many hymnals have indexes in the back or companion volumes that help the user match hymns to scripture passages or topics.]

h. Fill in the Blanks. In order to help the learners focus on the content of the biblical passage, at the beginning of the session ask each member of the group to read the biblical passage and fill out a brief questionnaire about the details of the passage (provide a copy for each learner or write the questions on the board). For example, if you are studying the unit in the IBS *Matthew* volume on Matthew 22:1–14, the questionnaire could include questions such as the following:

—In this story, Jesus compares the kingdom of heaven to what?

—List the various responses of those who were invited to the king's banquet but who did not come.

—When his invitation was rejected, how did the king feel? What did the king do?

—In the second part of the story, when the king saw a man at the banquet without a wedding garment, what did the king say? What did the man say? What did the king do?

—What is the saying found at the end of this story?

Gather the group's responses to the questions perhaps encourage discussion. Then lead the group through the IBS material helping the learners to understand the meanings of these details and the significance of the passage for today. Feeling creative? Instead of a fill-in-the blanks questionnaire, create a crossword puzzle from names and words in the biblical passage.

i. Get the Picture. In this approach, stimulate group discussion by incorporating a painting, photograph, or other visual object into the lesson. You can begin by having the group examine and comment on this visual or you can introduce the visual later in the lesson—it depends on the object used. If, for example, you are studying the unit Exodus 3:1–4:17 in the IBS *Exodus* volume, you may want to view Paul Koli's very colorful painting *The Burning Bush*. Two sources for this painting are *The Bible Through Asian Eyes*, edited by Masao Takenaka and Ron O'Grady (National City, Calif.: Pace Publishing Co., 1991), and *Imaging the Word: An Arts and Lectionary Resource,* vol. 3, edited by Susan A. Blain (Cleveland: United Church Press, 1996).

j. Now Hear This. Especially if your class is large, you may want to use the lecture method. As the teacher, you prepare a presentation on the biblical passage, using as many resources as you have available plus your own experience, but following the content of the IBS unit as a guide. You can make the lecture even more lively by asking the learners at various points along the way to refer to the visuals and quotes found in the "sidebars." A place can be made for questions (like the ones at the end of the unit)— either at the close of the lecture or at strategic points along the way.

> "It is . . . important to call a Bible study group back to what the text being discussed actually says, especially when an individual has gotten off on some tangent." —Richard Robert Osmer, *Teaching for Faith: A Guide for Teachers of Adult Classes* (Louisville, Ky.: Westminster John Knox Press, 1992), 71.

3. Keep These Teaching Tips in Mind

There are no surefire guarantees for a teaching success. However, the following suggestions can increase the chances for a successful study:

a. Always Know Where the Group Is Headed. Take ample time beforehand to prepare the material. Know the main points of the study, and know the destination. Be flexible, and encourage discussion, but don't lose sight of where you are headed.

131

b. Ask Good Questions; Don't Be Afraid of Silence. Ideally, a discussion blossoms spontaneously from the reading of the scripture. But more often than not, a discussion must be drawn from the group members by a series of well-chosen questions. After asking each question, give the group members time to answer. Let them think, and don't be threatened by a season of silence. Don't feel that every question must have an answer, and that as leader, you must supply every answer. Facilitate discussion by getting the group members to cooperate with each other. Sometimes, the original question can be restated. Sometimes it is helpful to ask a follow-up question like "What makes this a hard question to answer?"

Ask questions that encourage explanatory answers. Try to avoid questions that can be answered simply "Yes" or "No." Rather than asking, "Do you think Moses was frightened by the burning bush?" ask, "What do you think Moses was feeling and experiencing as he stood before the burning bush?" If group members answer with just one word, ask a follow-up question like "Why do you think this is so?" Ask questions about their feelings and opinions, mixed within questions about facts or details. Repeat their responses or restate their response to reinforce their contributions to the group.

> "Studies of learning reveal that while people remember approximately 10% of what they hear, they remember up to 90% of what they say. Therefore, to increase the amount of learning that occurs, increase the amount of talking about the Bible which each member does."—Roberta Hestenes, *Using the Bible in Groups* (Philadelphia: Westminster Press, 1983), 17.

Most studies can generate discussion by asking open-ended questions. Depending on the group, several types of questions can work. Some groups will respond well to content questions that can be answered from reading the IBS comments or the biblical passage. Others will respond well to questions about feelings or thoughts. Still others will respond to questions that challenge them to new thoughts or that may not have exact answers. Be sensitive to the group's dynamic in choosing questions.

Some suggested questions are: What is the point of the passage? Who are the main characters? Where is the tension in the story? Why does it say (this)_____, and not (that) _____? What raises questions for you? What terms need defining? What are the new ideas? What doesn't make sense? What bothers or troubles you about this passage? What keeps you from living the truth of this passage?

c. Don't Settle for the Ordinary. There is nothing like a surprise. Think of special or unique ways to present the ideas of the study. Upset the applecart of the ordinary. Even though the passage may be familiar, look for ways to introduce suspense. Remember that a little mystery can capture the imagination. Change your routine.

Along with the element of surprise, humor can open up a discussion. Don't be afraid to laugh. A well-chosen joke or cartoon may present the central theme in a way that a lecture would have stymied.

Sometimes a passage is too familiar. No one speaks up because everyone feels that all that could be said has been said. Choose an unfamiliar translation from which to read, or if the passage is from a Gospel, compare the story across two or more Gospels and note differences. It is amazing what insights can be drawn from seeing something strange in what was thought to be familiar.

d. Feel Free to Supplement the IBS Resources with Other Material. Consult other commentaries or resources. Tie in current events with the lesson. Scour newspapers or magazines for stories that touch on the issues of the study. Sometimes the lyrics of a song, or a section of prose from a well-written novel will be just the right seasoning for the study.

e. And Don't Forget to Check the Web. Check out our site on the World Wide Web (keyword "Interpretation Bible Studies" at www.ppcpub.org). Several possibilities for applying the teaching methods suggested above for individual IBS units will be available. Feel free to read, print, or download this material.

f. Stay Close to the Biblical Text. Don't forget that the goal is to learn the Bible. Return to the text again and again. Avoid making the mistake of reading the passage only at the beginning of the study, and then wandering away to comments on top of comments from that point on. Trust in the power and presence of the Holy Spirit to use the truths of the passage to work within the lives of the study participants.

> "The Bible is literature, but it is much more than literature. It is the holy book of Jews and Christians, who find there a manifestation of God's presence." —Kathleen Norris, *The Psalms* (New York: Riverhead Books, 1997), xxii.

What If I Am Using IBS in Personal Bible Study?

If you are using IBS in your personal Bible study, you can experiment and explore a variety of ways. You may choose to read straight through the study without giving any attention to the sidebars or other features. Or you may find yourself interested in a question or unfamiliar with a key term, and you can allow the sidebars," "Want to Know More?" and "Questions for Reflection" to lead you into deeper learning on these issues. Perhaps you will want to have a few commentaries or a Bible dictionary available to pursue what interests you. As was suggested in one of the teaching methods above, you may want to begin with the questions at the end, and then read the Bible passage followed by the IBS material. Trust the IBS resources to provide good and helpful information, and then follow your interests!

Want to Know More?

About leading Bible study groups? See Roberta Hestenes, *Using the Bible in Groups* (Philadelphia: Westminster Press, 1983).

About basic Bible content? See Duncan S. Ferguson, *Bible Basics: Mastering the Content of the Bible* (Louisville, Ky.: Westminster John Knox Press, 1995); William M. Ramsay, *The Westminster Guide to the Books of the Bible* (Louisville, Ky.: Westminster John Knox Press, 1994).

About the development of the Bible? See John Barton, *How the Bible Came to Be* (Louisville, Ky.: Westminster John Knox Press, 1997).

About the meaning of difficult terms? See Donald K. McKim, *Westminster Dictionary of Theological Terms* (Louisville, Ky.: Westminster John Knox Press, 1996); Paul J. Achtemeier, *Harper's Bible Dictionary* (San Francisco: Harper & Row, 1985).

For more information about IBS,

search under the keyword

"Interpretation Bible Studies" at

www.ppcpub.org